BEING LAURA

*The inspirational true story
of Laura O'Donnell*
*Actress, Stuntwoman, Entrepreneur
& Single Mum of five!*

Laura O'Donnell
and Jacqueline Haigh

CONTENTS

THE TURNING POINT

There is nothing more exhilarating than living your dreams and seeing your ambitions unfold – riding into a Viking village preparing to fight, doing stunts in films and on TV, and acting with celebrities is all part of it. So is helping a teenager overcome an eating disorder and showing people a way out of toxic relationships - being free to do whatever you want in your life and living the dreams that YOU want to live.

I can clearly remember the moment that my ambitions got shelved. I was only about ten years old. It was one of those typical British, drizzly Sunday afternoons in the 1990s. I'd been playing out in the garden, as usual; climbing trees, hula-hooping, or whacking the swing ball as hard as I could. Then it started pouring with rain, so I ran inside.

I would rather have been outside playing - being active was what I really enjoyed. So I slouched upstairs and flopped on the chair in my bedroom as I switched on the TV. There was an old American show playing, filmed over a decade before I was born. It starred three stunning women; one blonde and two brunettes with flared jumpsuits, long hair and killer, flicked fringes. But they weren't just sitting around looking good; they were doing martial arts, sorting out gangsters and being sassy as hell.

Instantly, I was hooked. I saw them as the perfect women; super strong and gorgeous too – like ninja goddesses! *They can really look after themselves*, I thought. *They can handle whatever life throws at them.* I wanted to be just like them; beautiful yes, but with strength and skills. Not just a pretty face.

The show was, of course, *Charlies Angels*. I sat on my bed and watched it until the very end, glued to the screen. As the credits scrolled down, the names of those three women came up on the screen – Jaclyn Smith, Farah Fawcett, and Kate Jackson. But alongside the names of the actors, director and cameramen, another credit caught my eye, 'Stuntwoman.'

What on earth was that? I'd never seen that word before. Although the internet was in its infancy at the time, I still went to our big, croaky family PC to see what I could find out.

"Stuntwoman … a woman who doubles for an actress during the filming of stunts and dangerous scenes," it said.

This was getting better by the minute! I felt the blood pumping around my body and a rush of adrenalin. Finally, I knew exactly what I wanted to do with my life and, for the first time, I felt excited about becoming an adult and doing a job. At that moment, my mum called me down for dinner. As I sat at the table and chomped on my Sunday roast, I told my family what I'd just watched.

"I want to do what Charlie's Angels do," I raved between mouthfuls of chicken. "I want to be a stuntwoman!"

I stopped eating for a moment and waited for the response. I expected my mum to throw her arms around me in excitement, maybe even call Hollywood straight away!

There was silence for a moment. Then Mum just laughed.

"That's not a job for a woman," she said. "Only men do that."

My fairy tale was starting to evaporate before my very eyes.

"But I've just seen them on TV," I protested. "If they can do it, why can't I?"

"You just can't," Mum snapped.

"Okay, I'm going to be an actress then," I declared. "Girls definitely do that!"

Mum looked exasperated at my dad, who took a deep breath and sighed.

"It's not possible," he explained with sad eyes, as if he was telling me that we couldn't get a puppy. "You're not going to be an actress; you'll never succeed in that. You need to pick another career that you'll be able to do instead."

Now my bubble was well and truly burst. I ate the rest of my dinner in silence. Afterwards, I asked to excuse myself from the table and ran up to my room. I sank onto my bed and started crying.

All my newfound dreams were crushed – what was the point of my life now? I had found my true calling and it had been snatched away from me before I could even enjoy the idea. If I couldn't be one of Charlie's Angels, I didn't want to do anything. I kept sobbing until I finally fell asleep. After that, I just believed in what my parents had said. I gave up hope. I guess I was stuck in that mindset and knew that was not good enough, had no chance, and could expect nothing from life.

Cut to twenty years later, as they say in the movies. I was thirty now, a single mum with five kids, working as a nurse in the local hospital. It was nearly Christmas, and I was flicking through the TV channels with my kids when the 2000 film version of *Charlie's Angels* came on. It had long since been my favourite movie; I must have watched it dozens of times – subconsciously craving that moment of freedom I had felt thinking that I could do something like that. I could even recite it line for line.

As it got to the best bit, when the girls were doing some kick-ass martial arts, my eyes welled up with tears. My kids saw me crying and asked me what was wrong. I told them that I'd always wanted to be an actress and a stuntwoman, but my parents told me it was possible.

"This is my passion," I whispered to them, as if frightened someone might overhear us, not even knowing if they would really understand. "This is what I have always wanted to do," I said it so quietly, so scared that I would once again be shut down.

The room went quiet again, just as it did all those years ago with my parents. I waited for a painful heartbeat, half expecting my kids to also dash my dreams.

Then my eldest Shannon walked up to me and put her arms around me. "I love you, Mum," she said. "I'll support you."

"Yeah, we all want to help you," the others chimed in. "You can do it!"

They all closed around me for a big group hug, which we always did in our family. It felt like a key had turned inside me, something unlocked, and I woke up the next day with a new sense of purpose and determination.

Right, that's it! I decided. I'm going for it!

With that decision, a ball of energy burst out of my heart and through my whole body, lighting me up from the inside. I remembered an old saying I'd read somewhere years before, which had always struck me. It was a quote from the 18th century German writer Johann Wolfgang von Goethe.

"The moment one definitely commits oneself then providence moves too. All sorts of things occur to help one that would never otherwise have occurred ... Unforeseen incidents, meetings, and material assistance, which no man could have dreamed would have come his way."

Well, Johann, you can say that again!

This was the moment that I definitely committed to my mission and sure enough, as soon as I did, everything started to change in my life to help me. Almost instantly, I started to meet people and find myself in places that would all take me a step further to my lifelong goal.

Call it luck, call it destiny; whatever it was, I was so grateful. Of course, that doesn't mean it was easy, far from it. This decision was just the beginning of what has been a long and challenging road, difficult but amazing, hilarious and unforgettable all at once. But knowing that the kids were on my side and would support me made all the difference. With the right friends and family in life, you can achieve anything.

These days, I'm proud to say that I am a successful actress, stuntwoman and life coach, as well as a single mum to five wonderful kids. My life wasn't always like this though. I've suffered times of hell and been terribly bullied. I was stuck in a pattern of being used and abused– I hit rock bottom and nearly gave up - but that's all behind me now. I'm sharing my story to show that, no matter what life throws at us, we can overcome our struggles and fulfil our dreams. We are all beautiful, powerful beings and can manifest wonderful, inspiring lives that we love. The journey starts with our desire and the bravery to take that very first step and become 'un-stuck'.

ONE GIANT LEAP

The day after rewatching *Charlie's Angels*, age thirty, I quit my job. At the time, I worked at the local hospital in Wrexham where I lived. I'd been a nurse for two years by this point; before that, I was a carer. I just fell into the job really. It was never what I really wanted to do, but it was a safety net, the kind of industry where I could always find work. I needed that security because it was just me and the children and I had to be able to provide for them. Unfortunately, their fathers were not very helpful with any of that.

I had enjoyed aspects of being a nurse. I genuinely liked looking after people and helping them get better. I've always loved caring for others; if I can help anyone, I always will. But the job didn't turn out to be what I expected. The workload was ridiculous; we were chronically understaffed, doing fourteen or fifteen-hour shifts every day. It was so hard to deal with the number of patients coming in. We were treated badly too, always taken for granted by patients and the other staff. Plus, the childcare at the hospital was so expensive that, despite all the hours I was working, I had barely anything left at the end of the month.

I can still remember that morning everything changed. In each bay in the ward, you had beds for six patients and a TV on the wall. So, I was sitting there, Richard and Judy blaring away in the background, writing up notes about the patients and what had happened that morning.

Well, my body was there but my mind was somewhere else entirely. I was always daydreaming about the children and I living in LA, being celebrities, or touring the world as a family with some sort of show. I was fantasising about my future life like this when the call bell rang and snapped me back to reality. I looked around; unfortunately, I wasn't in Beverly Hills but still at Wrexham hospital!

Then the other nurse on the ward came over and nudged me.

"Come on, Laura," she said. "We've got to go."

Oh, okay, back to the job, I thought.

I went to help get a patient washed. As I walked into the room, he sat up. He was a rugby player who'd had to have a knee replacement. It was such a shame; he was only about twenty-five. This was a specialist orthopaedic hospital, so we looked after a lot of professional footballers and sportsmen like him.

The guy was lying in bed with his leg in a cushioned vice. When he realised that I was going to be washing him, he was very embarrassed. I reassured him that I'd seen many naked men in my job, and there was nothing to be shy about.

I bent down to the left of him and started to wash his leg. Because he was in a cast near to his groin, I had to wash around there too. Then, as I was rinsing him down, he got an erection. He didn't say anything, but he went bright red, poor thing!

Nurses are used to seeing that all the time in our line of work, but he was really nervous and didn't know what to say. It was funny really but, of course, I couldn't start laughing. To distract him, I tried to make conversation about the first thing I could think of. Because he lived locally, I knew his whole family, so I asked about them.

"How's your mum?" I said. "She was in here last week."

The young guy looked horrified at that and went an even brighter shade of scarlet. Afterwards, I realised this was the most inappropriate thing to say in the circumstances and just made it even worse!

Then, after I'd finished washing his leg, as I was trying to put his stocking back on, I got caught in the drip line wire. At that moment, the sister nurse and the doctor came in to observe the patients. From where they were standing, it looked like I was sucking his cock!

As you can imagine, this made him even more embarrassed. *Oh God*, I thought. *I need to get out of here.*

I jerked up but, as I moved the tray line table out of the way, I twisted my back. A huge pain shot up my spine and I couldn't move.

So, there I was bent over next to his erection; the nurse is telling me to stand up but I'm trying to explain that I can't because I've pulled my back!

For God's sake, I'm such a clutz! Why do these things always happen to me? Of course, the other nurse and doctor knew there was nothing going on, but it looked awful. After that, I managed to disentangle myself and the others attended to him. I left the room, but my back was killing me. I hobbled up to the office and sat in a chair to rest.

I'm only young and I've already pulled my back, I thought. The bottom of my foot had also swollen from walking on the hard floors for hours every day. I'd even had steroid injections in my feet to be able to walk. *If I stay in this job, I'm going to be crippled by the time I'm 40!*

You often heard nurses complaining about the toll the work took on their bodies; how they had major problems with their feet and backs and had often done irreparable damage by age forty. Plus, we had nurses off with stress all the time. I remember one got suspended for giving a patient the wrong medication, but she was covering someone and had done three fourteen hour shifts in a row. Mistakes are made because everyone is tired; nurses are so overworked and underpaid it's insane.

"I can't do this anymore," I stood up and declared out loud.

What's the point of doing a job that you hate for the rest of your life? I thought. You only get one life. I might as well put in all that hard work to try to achieve my dreams.

So, I went to the office and told my boss. Afterwards, a wave of euphoria washed over me. I felt excited, although I was scared too.

What the hell am I going to do for money? I wondered as I drove home through the rainy streets. I've always worked, sometimes two or three jobs. I've never been on benefits or received much support from the kids' dads.

That night, I went home, and the children and I all sat down together. We got the popcorn out and had a family movie night. These were the times together that I loved the most.

The next day, I wanted to ask my friends what they thought. I invited them round for a Girls Night In, and my friend Karen suggested an Ann Summers party because she was working as a rep for them at the time.

"Why not?" I said. It had been a while since I'd done anything like that anyway!

So, that night, I had all the girls around. We had some snacks and a few bottles of Prosecco, then we started looking at these giant pink, double-end vibrators and throwing them about, falling about laughing. Karen had also brought loads of sexy outfits, which we tried on, like a French maid and a policewoman. There was even a nurse's uniform, but I wasn't about to try that on. I was never dressing like a nurse again as long as I lived, not even in the bedroom!

After about an hour of this hilarity, I sat my friends down and told them that I had something to say.

"I've quit my job," I announced. "I'm going to become a stuntwoman and an actress!"

At first, they laughed. But when they looked at the determination on my face, they released that I was serious.

"You can't do that, Laura," they said. "What if you get hurt? You're a beautiful girl, and you don't want to mess up your looks."

"I can't let the fear of that stop me," I insisted. "I've wanted to do this all my life. Now's the time that I have to just go for it."

For all she's a crazy party animal, my friend Karen is also very sensible. She asked me how I was going to make it work practically. We spoke about what I would do for money while I trained as, of course, I still had bills to pay and children to look after.

However, I'd thought all this through already.

"I'm going to work 16 hours per week and train the rest," I announced. "I know it isn't going to be easy. Things will be tight, but I know I can do it."

As I spoke my intention out loud again, I could feel the energy build inside me, along with the overriding sense that I must follow through.

"Sounds very risky to me," Karen warned.

She was my best friend and couldn't help worrying about me, but she could tell that I'd already made up my mind.

"You seem pretty set on this," she added.

"Whenever I speak about it, I get this feeling in my stomach, like a burning excitement," I explained. "I just know that this is meant for me."

Karen paused for a moment, then stood up and flung her arms around me.

"Well, you have so much passion for this, of course you can achieve it?"

She opened the last bottle of Prosecco, and they toasted my new career.

Now I had my children's and my friends' support, I was ready to put my plan into action. The next morning, I lay in bed in my pyjamas, drinking a cup of tea, which my eldest Shannon had brought me. I switched on my laptop to find out exactly what I needed to do to become a stunt woman.

Suddenly, I heard laughing and joking from downstairs. I got up and went to see what was happening. As I approached the bottom of the stairs, I heard the door go. I opened up and it was the postman with a parcel for me.

"Hello," I said and took the pen to sign for it.

Then, from the living room, I hear Harvey shouting.

"Blake, Blake, there's a penis in your face!"

Embarrassed, I glanced at the postman, knowing that he'd heard it too. Then, the boys burst into the hallway, laughing their heads off.

And now I realise what they meant – after the Ann Summers party had ended, clearly not all of the vibrators had been packed away. One of the huge, pink ones got left behind and Harvey was smacking his brother around the face with it, yelling, "Blake, there's a penis in your face!"

The giant, pink dildo was flopping around all over the place and the boys were in hysterics.

I grabbed the vibrator as quickly as I could, whilst still trying to sign for the parcel. Fortunately, the postman just laughed.

"I can see you're having one of those mornings," he sniggered. "Bye lads!"

He smiled at the boys and went on his way, no doubt pleased to escape this madhouse! But nothing could affect my good mood that morning. Now my plan was set, and I was on my way.

ONCE UPON A TIME

So, there I was a single mum to five kids (13, 10, 7, 6 and 3), with no partner and now unemployed to boot! *How did it come to this?* I asked myself. I didn't expect things to turn out that way. But, as they say, life is what happens when you are making plans.

As a little girl, I thought being an adult would involve independence, travelling and seeing the world. I loved adventure and I was a very active child, full of energy. I was always in the woods, climbing trees or catching bees in nets. When I was just three years old, I showed my spirit of adventure by scrambling over my parents' fence at the back of our garden and rushed through the long corn in the farmer's field. Back then, all I wanted to be was a horse! I loved the freedom they had and how fast they could run. If I couldn't be a horse, I at least wanted to be a jockey.

I'm lucky to say that my early years were very happy. I was born in Great Yarmouth on 18 May 1984. Three years after my parents had moved down from Scotland to Lowestoft because of their work at the time. Dad was an accountant and Mum was a supervisor at the Birds Eye Wall's factory. They both still have Scottish accents and they used to go back there on holiday every summer.

My mum and dad were both extremely hard workers, but they were completely different in every other way. My father is a relaxed, laid-back man, who speaks softly and lets my mum deal with everything. He's 6 foot tall with a moustache and thick, black hair. My mum is the total opposite. She's only 4'10" but she's very strict; at the factory where she works, they call her Cranky Haggis!

I am the eldest of three sisters. My middle sister Stephanie is three years younger than me and has a completely different personality.

She's quiet, shy and very rational, like my mum, and works as a teacher for young children. We had a real rivalry when we were growing up; she'd pinch my stuff and get cross, then I'd nick hers. It was quite horrible but, hey, that's what sisters do, isn't it?

My other sister Nathalie is five years younger than me. She's very laid back like my dad and works as a paramedic. She didn't start speaking until she was about four because Stephanie and I would do all the talking; Nathalie would just point, and we'd speak for her. We used to do lots of activities together and we're a very musical family; my dad plays guitar, and my cousins sing. We used to all sit down and have sing songs when we got together, it was such fun.

But then, at five years old, everything changed. When I started school, I was badly bullied.

From the age of five when I started primary school, I felt that a lot of people didn't like me. I'm not sure exactly why but it was probably just because of the way I looked. Unfortunately, I was a very ugly child. At least I was always told that by people. I was chubby with lots of freckles and thick, black hair with tight curls like that style old ladies have when they get perms.

Everyone teased me all the time and called me 'Freckle Face' and 'Poodle Head'. I didn't have any friends in the classroom. One day when I was about seven, I was crying at my desk.

"What's wrong?" the teacher asked.

"No one likes me," I replied through my tears.

To prove me wrong, the teacher took my hand and stood me up in front of all thirty children in class. Everyone was looking at me; it was so humiliating.

"Who likes Laura?" the teacher asked.

No one put up their hand or even made eye contact with me! My heart sank, I was so upset. I didn't even tell my parents when I got home; I was too mortified. In fact, I didn't tell anyone until I was a grown woman. The secret burned in my heart for many years.

Another time aged seven, my grandparents bought a beautiful doll which I adored. I was playing with the other kids in my street and took out my doll to show everyone but then my mum called me in for tea. The next morning, I realised that I'd left my doll in the park and rushed out to find it. But it had been ripped to shreds, it's stuffing strewn everywhere. I was heartbroken and couldn't stop crying for hours.

Another time, I was playing in the park with those same kids, wearing my favourite yellow dress. One girl got a bag of blackberries and pushed my head inside it, so the blackberries went all over my face and stained my best dress.

It wasn't just girls that bullied me either. Once, when I was in the library, for no apparent reason a boy announced that I was horrible and he didn't like me, then smacked my head on the table and kicked me, hard. All this just because I was there.

For some reason, people were always beating me up. When I was aged ten, I started to play the electric guitar. My dad played the guitar so I thought I would take it up and learnt to play Oasis. My music teacher heard me play and suggested that I perform in the school concert with some of the boys - and because we had something in common, they at least started to like me. But then, because the popular lads now spoke to me, the popular girls didn't like it - even though I was no threat to them. One day, I was walking up to the local chip shop near my house when one of these girls came up and smacked the chips out of my hand and told me to stay away from the boys. The chip shop owner knew my mum so called her to come and collect me.

At that time, I had a friend called Sally, who was one of the pretty kids. We both had a crush on the same boy, so we decided to get him Valentines cards. When she gave him her card, he looked delighted and read it straight away. When I gave him mine, he smirked at her then ripped it up in front of my face. How humiliating!

My sisters and I would also get teased because our parents were strict Catholics. They called us Bible Bashers and laughed at us for going to Sunday school. I was confirmed too and went to all the classes with the vicar. However, I wasn't sure what to believe; I didn't really have any faith. I'd had such bad luck through my whole short life. Even If I did pray to God when I was getting bullied, it didn't make any difference. I felt like there wasn't any hope or anyone looking out for me Up There or anywhere else.

Despite this, when I was eleven, I became a bell ringer in the local church and went to practise every Thursday night. I got even more stick for that, of course, but I liked hanging around with the older people there. They were gentle and encouraged me all the time.

"Well done, you're doing great on the bells," they'd declare. "It's so nice to have a young face here too."

They might not be cool but at least my fellow bell ringers didn't make me feel worthless.

As a youth, I would sit in my room and try to figure out what I had done wrong for people not to like me. It was the worst feeling in the world, that sense that you don't fit in anywhere. I didn't understand why it was happening either because I was a genuinely nice person who would talk to anyone. Looking back, maybe that's why I wanted to be a Charlie's Angel; they were tough and looked like they were never beaten up. Maybe deep down, that's why I wanted to be a stuntwoman too.

I started horse riding and dancing around that time too. I really liked any sport; I was quite a tom boy and always dressed in baggy training gear. I loved swimming and played squash and badminton with my dad. The coach was very impressed with my squash and even said that I could be a world champion player if I kept it up. When I told Dad, he was so proud of me. However, I wasn't doing well academically at school because I was always daydreaming. When sitting in class, my mind would be drifting off, thinking, *why can't I be someone else?* Or I'd be conjuring up ways I could get people to like me. But, of course, it never worked.

Growing up, I never really felt at home in my skin. I always had the feeling that, wherever I was, I wasn't meant to be there. I always knew that the moment I could leave, I would. I remember watching *The Hills* as a young girl; my life-long dreams of moving to LA started around then.

How lucky these people are, I thought. I longed for the freedom of their lives and the way that they could do whatever they wanted. *How I'd love to go there.*

In year five of middle school, aged eight, I had my first ever drama lesson. We filed into the class and sat down then the teacher called our names.

"O'Donnell," Mr Walsh said. "Are you Irish?"

"No, sir, I'm Scottish."

That made him laugh. Here we go, I thought. Someone else is going to start teasing me now, but then the class started, and everything changed. When we became a character and spoke dialogue, it felt fantastic. The excitement at transforming myself was huge. When I was acting, I didn't feel nervous. I didn't even feel like me; it was like being a different person.

It was such an extraordinary change to go from being bullied so drastically then be in a lesson where I felt free and didn't care about what other people thought of me. Once, we got into a group of four and came up with a scene in which we were performing a game show. I got all of the class really involved until they were standing up and cheering. *I created that*, I thought with joy. *That was me!*

In another lesson, I was teamed up with the popular kids. We did a scene where we had to look across the room and stare into each other's eyes. I was playing a beautiful woman and had to gaze at the boy opposite me. At that moment, I lost my shyness and became that beautiful character. I felt totally accepted – at least until the end of class.

Finally, I had found something that I enjoyed and could be respected for. The one thing that people said I was good at was drama. Unlike so many of my other teachers, Mr Walsh was fun and very laid back. I felt safe in his class like he wasn't going to shout at me or tell me off.

Mr Walsh taught me drama for about three years. Then I moved to high school, although I still used to go back and visit him. My younger sisters were at the middle school, so when I went to see them in their school play, I would have a chat with Mr Walsh.

One time, I told him that I wanted to be an actress.

"That's great," he exclaimed. "You should go for it!"

I left the school that day flying on air. His encouragement was like a warm glow wrapped around me. It seemed like he was the only person in the world that understood me and although his encouragement was not enough at the time to unstick me from my now ingrained belief that I couldn't do it - I will still be grateful to him for the rest of my life.

GETTING TOUGH

Even though I was now a grown woman of thirty, Mr Walsh's kind words still rang in my ears the day after I resigned from nursing. That afternoon, I collected the kids from nursery, brought them home and fed them. Then we all sat down together, fired up the computer and started to do some research. I wanted to include them right from the start of my new journey and make this something we did as a family.

So, how am I going to do this? I wondered. Where on earth do I start?

At a loss for any better idea, I typed "how to be a stunt woman" into the internet. Ah, good old Google! Straight away there were countless things that you could do and courses to take you down this path less travelled. Before long, I found myself on the home page of the British Stunt Register. Dating back to 1973, this esteemed organisation was founded to establish the highest standards of performance and safety for stunt performers, actors and crew. Their website outlined the Stunt Grading Scheme, which aimed "to create true professionals capable of meeting the challenges faced by stunt performers and coordinators in the 21st Century."

The British Stunt Register gave a full description of how to begin a career as a stunt performer and get into the industry. In order to qualify for membership, you had to reach the required standard in a minimum of six disciplines. The first group of skills was called "Fighting" and included martial arts like Taekwondo, karate and Kung Fu, and other fighting sports like wrestling and boxing.

Group B was called "Falling" and included trampolining and gymnastics, both of which I had some experience in. Group C was "Riding and Driving", including horse-riding and stunt driving cars.

And so, it went on. Blimey, it would take me years to learn all this! And it was going to be expensive – it costs a lot to train. I knew it wasn't going to be easy, but I was determined to find a way.

Because I was good on horses anyway, I decided to start with stunt riding. I went onto Facebook and asked around to see if anyone knew an appropriate trainer. Some contacts led me to a massively well-known stuntman; he'd been in a lot of the top films and worked extensively with Robbie Williams. I messaged him and we got talking. He was very busy at the time but a nice guy and promised to help me when he was back from working in Spain.

I was impatient though and couldn't wait. Big mistake! I went back to Google and found a trainer in Wales called Toby. I told the well-known stuntman and asked if he knew him.

"Not recommended," he told me. "Avoid at all costs!"

However, I was keen to get started and Toby was the only person available, so I didn't listen.

I booked a week to stay in a hotel close to Toby's stables to learn stunt horse riding. It cost £500 for the week's course. *I can't afford that!* I thought. *I've got five kids and I'm not working.* But I was so determined to get started, I scrimped and saved and got the money together to sign up.

When the big day arrived, I drove to Snowdonia, super excited. I stayed overnight in a nearby hotel then the next morning we got started.

For the first hour, it was okay, but we were very much going back to basics.

"You need to learn how to ride again," Toby declared.

"Why?" I asked.

By this stage, I'd been riding and jumping for over fifteen years. I'd even had my own horses.

"You're not doing it right," he explained.

Oh well, he was the teacher, so I had to trust that he knew what he was doing.

That morning, we went through all the basics. Then, in the afternoon, I had another hour's lesson.

"Now, you can muck out the horses," Toby announced.

"Why?" I protested. "I'm supposed to have a morning and afternoon training session."

But he wouldn't budge and sent me packing to the stables.

"You're not ready to do stunts," he declared. "You just have to work."

WTF? I was paying a lot of money for this 'teaching'. I had mucked out countless times when I was young, but I had never had to pay for the privilege.

I did as I was told and mucked out the horses, but I was starting to get annoyed. This wasn't going to get me any closer to becoming a stunt woman. I hoped that things would improve, but, when the evening came, Toby had another demand for me.

"Come to my apartment," he said.

I didn't like the way this was going.

"No thanks," I muttered.

"Come on," he insisted.

He told me that there was another girl staying at his flat and she was bisexual.

"Molly fancies you," he revealed.

"What?" I snapped. "That's completely irrelevant!"

This was all starting to get a bit dodgy. I was on my own in the middle of nowhere with this guy, with no one around to help.

But Toby wasn't taking no for an answer.

"We're going to have a film night," he continued. "Have a drink."

"I don't drink."

Luckily, I'm not a drinker. And I definitely didn't feel like I owed him one, when I was paying the guy to teach me!

"Go on," he drooled. "I think we should get together."

Then he told me about how all the girls in the stunt business have threesomes. It got worse and worse. In the end, I snapped.

"I've had enough," I shouted. "I'm going back to the hotel."

I marched back to my room and slammed the door. As I lay down on the bed, I felt awful. I'd had such high hopes for this training, and this is how it had turned out.

The next day, there was no mention of the offer of drinks or Molly. In fact, Toby acted as though nothing had happened at all.

Yet again, my "teacher" made me trot around the yard to learn the basics. Finally, I was so annoyed, I confronted him.

"I've paid you all this money to learn trick riding," I cried. "When are we going to do some stunts?"

"You're not ready," he sneered. "You need to get to know the horse."

"What are you on about?" I protested. I didn't have time to do that. I was only supposed to be there a week!

Of course, I knew what this was really about. Toby was the type of guy that gets angry if you argue with him or turn him down. We've all met that type. Someone who feels inadequate (possibly because he was only 5'2") and tries to overcompensate with overly aggressive and sometimes predatory behaviour.

After playing it so cool all day, that night the same thing happened. Toby asked me to come for a drink and when I refused, he got nasty and tore me apart. It looked to me like he was projecting all his shit onto me to make himself feel better.

"You're useless," he jeered. "You've got no talent at all."

It was clear he was trying to make me feel small and doubt my ability.

"You'll never get on the register unless you sleep with me," he continued. "You're just a pretty, little blonde girl with big tits, and five spoilt brats. No one will ever take you seriously."

I'd heard this jibe about my body many times before. It's a good job I was thick-skinned from what I had already been through. These days, I don't care about having large breasts. I really couldn't give a toss; I call them my big udders! They've fed five bloody kids after all!

You get to that stage where you're not bothered about what people say. But, of course, it wasn't always like that. Women often think they want big boobs; indeed, some ladies spend a fortune to get them. But it's not always as great as you think. Like I said, I was a bit of a tom boy when I was growing up and had a chubby, androgynous figure.

Then one summer, all that changed. The August before I started high school, my boobs grew quite big. I was a C cup at age thirteen. I completely transformed over the six-week holidays. I spent a lot of time with my friend Gemma and her mum was always out so we would never really eat, and I lost a lot of weight. By the time I started high school, I was really slim with big boobs. I started to get noticed then. When we were doing sports on the high school pitch, all the boys would look at me. And, for obvious reasons, I hated running!

If we were doing PE, a lot of boys wanted to partner up with me. They used to make all those bouncy, bouncy gestures, jiggling their hands up and down. It was so humiliating. I carried on with my games at first but then I even stopped playing squash. Although I loved sports, it got to the point where I refused to do it at school because of all the attention I attracted.

I got the nickname Lara Croft because of my black hair and big boobs. I loathed it. I used to try and tape my breasts down with masking tape and always wore tight bras. In a way, I felt like they took away my freedom; the freedom of being a child, rather than a sexualised woman.

One day in the playground, a boy came around behind me and grabbed my chest. I kicked him so hard in the balls that he had to go home because he was in so much pain. And do you know the cheek of it? I was the one who got told off for kicking him, even though he shouldn't have been groping me in the first place. Somehow it wasn't his fault!

The boy who beat me up in middle school did apologise from the bottom of his heart when he was older. But regardless of how much bullies say sorry later, you never really get over it; you still carry around that childhood pain inside of you. But to anyone being bullied, I say, the tide will turn. Just ignore the haters and focus on your own life and dreams. The amount of people from school that now follow me on Instagram is ridiculous. People who were horrible to me back then suddenly want to be my best friend. I get it all the time. I see them sometimes when I go back to visit my parents.

"I didn't recognise you, you're so good looking," they coo and smile as if that makes everything okay.

How ridiculous. As if this makes all those years of cruelty instantly vanish.

"We follow you now because you're pretty," they gush. "You turned really fit, you did."

Cheers for that, buddy. Wish I could say the same for you!

So, Toby mocking me about my boobs was just another in a long line of males who'd done that since childhood. But I was older now and wasn't going to stand for it anymore. There was no way I was going to let this egomaniac treat me like that; I didn't need to be in this toxic environment.

I told Toby where to shove his riding crop and left. I didn't even ask for my money back; I just wanted to get away from him.

As I got in my car and drove home, I felt devastated. *What a terrible start to my training,* I thought. *What a huge waste of time and money.* I should have listened to the professionals and stayed well clear of Toby. I vowed to make sure I followed good advice next time.

STRIKE A POSE

I wish I could say that this experience with Toby was the first time when the men around me tried to exploit their professional position for sex. By this point in my life I had kind of got used to it. I remember a time when I was about nineteen. My first daughter Shannon was two years old. She was with her dad, so I'd popped out to get some bits at the supermarket.

I took my time walking around the aisles, so I didn't forget anything, then went to the till. After I'd paid and left the shop, a stocky man in his forties approached me.

"I've been following you around Sainsbury's," he announced.

Okay ... Well, what do you say to that? I felt a bit freaked out by him, to be honest. It seemed creepy.

"I see," I replied, hesitantly. "Is that for any particular reason?"

He flipped into professional mode and took a business card out of his pocket.

"Well, actually, I'm a photographer," he explained. "I think you're very attractive and, by looking at you, you'll be photogenic, so I'd like to do some pictures with you."

I took his card and said I would think about it.

When I got home, I had a look at his work online and they were actually quite nice pictures; there was nothing vulgar or anything revealing. At the time, there was an online forum called Purple Port where people could leave feedback on the photographers. Several models that had previously worked with him commented on the shoot. The girls all said that he made them feel comfortable and he was professional and not sleazy at all.

As I looked at all the models that he had worked with, they were stunning, and all my old inferiority complexes came up again. *Why on earth would anyone want to photograph me?* I thought. *There's no way I'm good enough for this.*

This wasn't actually the first time I'd done modelling. When I was sixteen, I had a picture taken of me with a veil on for a local billboard. It was for an advert so there was a buy-out fee and I even got paid £1500 – a small fortune for me back then. Because I still had it in my head from childhood that I was ugly, it was a bit strange to be asked to model. But then, when I saw how well the pictures had turned out, I was amazed. It was quite shocking and highlighted the difference in how I saw myself to how other people saw me.

I loved the way that I seemed like a different character in the picture, just like in acting, and the mysterious way the camera tells a story about you just by looking at your face. Now, here I was, three years later, being asked to model again. Being a young mum for the first time can really dent your confidence, but I didn't want to let my insecurity stop me. So, after I'd researched the photographer and decided he was kosher, I gave him a call.

We arranged to do a photo shoot in Chester. That afternoon, it was quite cold out, but I got in my car and set off. Driving to his studio, I had butterflies in my stomach and felt very nervous but also excited to be giving modelling another go. When I arrived at the studio, it was a very funky place. They had loads of cool props like umbrellas, coloured chairs, different outfits and backgrounds. I felt like a little kid, trying on the costumes and messing around with all the toys.

After careful consideration, I selected my first outfit, a very flattering, white dress. I got changed and came out into the studio and sat on a green sofa. The photographer started to shoot me, but I couldn't hide the fact that I was nervous. After he'd taken about twenty pictures, he showed me a few of them. Some were okay, but they were mostly coming out a bit stiff.

"Let's relax and have some fun," he said. "You're gorgeous, just be yourself."

Since then, I've learnt that the camera's always better when you're not actually concentrating on it. It's when you're having fun that you get the best photos, when you're not really posing as such. You start moving around, toss your head a bit and sway, and that energy comes out in the images. So, we took some more pictures and after a while he showed me them. Because I was relaxed now, and trusted this guy, they got better and better. The final pictures turned out wonderfully. They were stunning and very elegant. I couldn't believe it was really me.

Then one of the photographer's other models turned up. She was a size zero and had the tiniest frame. Even though I was only size eight, I was quite large compared to her. *She's so stunning,* I thought, my insecurities flooding back like a tsunami. *Why would he want to photograph me when he's got gorgeous, thin girls like that?*

I tried to shake off the feeling and focus on the job at hand. The model and I did a couple of pictures together. It was fun and the time soon went by. After the shoot, the girl and I were getting changed downstairs. When I saw her in her underwear, she looked so frail and fragile. She told me that she only ate once a day and that was just some wholegrain cereal or a protein shake. She'd never eat anything more substantial than that. Then she revealed that, even though she'd had no food, she would take lots of laxative chocolate to go to the bathroom before a shoot and even make herself sick.

I completely understood what this model was going through. I had been anorexic myself when I was fourteen because I got so depressed about my life. I had been so badly bullied that I was too shy to eat in front of other people in case I made a fool of myself, got food around my mouth or spilt something. I went down to under six and a half stone. I had so little energy from not eating that I was really tired and couldn't concentrate; I used to fall asleep in class all the time.

This went on for about three years. I only finally started eating normally again when I got pregnant. Then I found that I didn't care as much – things were different now and I wasn't at school anymore, thank God! Now it was actually quite nice to be feeding this new life inside of me.

So, although I thought this other model looked gorgeous, I could see how the industry had messed her up. I was excited to do more modelling, but I wanted to make sure that it didn't increase my insecurities to the point where it gave me an eating disorder. I definitely did not want to go back there.

Funnily enough, I tried laxative chocolate myself once when my second child Malachy was a baby. I had a piece, then left the rest of the bar in my bag and went to make him lunch. When I was in the kitchen, he went into my bag and took everything out, as kids do, and ate half the bar of chocolate.

When I realised what had happened, I phoned up the doctors.

"There's not much we can do about it now," they said, laughing. "It's going to come out one way or the other."

Oh my God, you can say that again! Not long afterwards, there was a nappy explosion that went on for about four hours.

After the shoot with the photographer, he put the pictures up on Purple Port and I got contacted by many other guys. Like a lot! They were asking what my rates and whether I would go topless, do full nude or implied nude, which is when you're naked, but you don't actually see anything. In my profile, my level was clothed or swimwear, but that was it. I wouldn't go any further.

Of course, that didn't stop the photographers trying it on.

"Would you do scenes with another girl or a guy?" they asked.

You must be kidding, I thought. That sounds more like porn!

"No, I definitely wouldn't do anything like that, thank you," I replied firmly, nipping that particular line of conversation in the bud.

So, in the weeks that followed, I started to do some more shoots. I got a few where they had agreed to clothed only online but when I turned up at the studio, they tried to pressure me to get naked.

"Not a chance," I declared and stuck to my resolve.

I wasn't going to be bullied about this.

Then, a really good photographer contacted me on Purple Port.

"Standard shoot is fine," he confirmed. "Fully clothed, no problem."

He didn't push me and made me feel comfortable straight away.

"I've got a project to do, and I think you'd look great as the front cover for a magazine cover," he explained.

He just wanted a picture of my face wearing a hat with a close up on my eyes.

He seemed nice, so I was looking forward to the shoot. When the day arrived, I turned up at the big studio feeling excited. He had a lot of gear; cameras, computers and lighting everywhere.

This looks like a good set-up, I thought. He's clearly got a lot of work going on.

When I saw how professional it was, I relaxed. We got the headshots with me wearing the hat and him close in on my face.

Afterwards, we had a look through the pictures, and they'd come out really well, even if I do say so myself!

"Well done," he declared. "You're a natural!"

I was so relieved. I was starting to feel like I could be good at this modelling lark. *Maybe I wasn't too ugly after all?*

"Right, now let's have some fun," the photographer announced. "Shall we do some pictures for your portfolio?"

"Thank you," I replied. "That would be great."

When they're starting out, models and actresses always need as many pictures as they can get, in different looks and outfits.

"So, what would you like to do?" he asked.

"I've got a couple of outfits with me. Let's try some of them."

I went upstairs and put on some white hotpants and a matching shirt. Then I came back down to the studio and sat on the floor with one leg crossed over the over.

The photographer started snapping away happily.

"These are really lovely pictures," he said. "Can you just undo a couple of buttons at the top, so you can get your shoulder out?"

Okay, I thought. I don't mind doing that. A bit of shoulder is fine.

He carried on taking the pictures then asked me to undo another button.

"Alright," I agreed. "Just one more."

He started shooting again but, after a few minutes, he came over to me and tried to pull my shirt even lower. *Here we go.*

"What are you doing?" I asked.

"Your shirt is in the way," he replied. "It would be nice if it went a bit lower."

Then he put his hands on my shoulders. Suddenly, my stomach lurched, and I started to feel sick.

"That's okay, I'm fine with what we've got now," I said, standing up.

"Are you sure? I'm just trying to get the nicest pictures for you," he justified. "I didn't mean to touch you like that; I was just trying to get a bit more for the camera."

"It's fine," I snapped, edging away.

Then I went downstairs, collected up my clothes and left. I was freaking out; it was just me and him all alone in that big studio. Why should I feel scared like that, just for the sake of a few shots? It wasn't worth putting myself in that predicament. It annoys me that women so often have to go through all this. Why can't we just be left alone to get on with the job?

So that day I gave up modelling, but, despite the experience with Toby the horse trainer, I wasn't going to give up becoming a stunt woman. I had finally embarked on pursuing my dream and I wasn't going to let some wanker stop me now!

To avoid a repetition of the previous experience, I decided to look for a female trainer instead. I put out a post on Facebook and someone told me about a woman called Nina who lived over in Hereford. I gave her a call and we clicked straight away. Nina is a lovely person, very strong-willed but very sweet. She's very pretty too; 5'6" with an athletic build and long brown hair. Like a real Charlie's Angel!

Nina explained that she was doing a five-day trick riding holiday with a bit of everything for a similar price to Toby's. But the similarity ended there; this was completely different. Straight away, I was cantering around doing stunts like vaulting. This is where you sit on the horse, which has a round, trick riding saddle on it, with a pommel – a stick in the middle, which you hold onto to get in and out of the tricks. I practised swinging underneath the horse's body, then pulled myself up on the other side of the horse.

After about two and a half hours, we had lunch. Then in the afternoon, we did another two and a half hours of trick riding. When I stood up on the saddle for the first time, it was amazing. I couldn't stop grinning.

"Wow, it's so high up here," I called out to Nina. "I feel like I'm flying!"

When you're galloping with the wind in your face, it's such an exciting feeling – pure freedom. I can't pretend that it isn't dangerous. If the horse changes direction at any point, you can easily come off and hurt yourself, so you have to plan your landings as best you can and know how to dismount. But fortune was smiling at me, and I didn't have any problems. Even to this day, I've had a close call a few times when I've slipped, but I've never fallen off. Fingers crossed it always stays that way.

This is it, I realised as I finally slowed down at the end of the day. *I'm really living my dream.* It was the best feeling in the world. As I returned the horse to the stable, I felt euphoric. Until the next day, that is.

When I work up in the morning, I couldn't move. I wasn't used to this amount of exercise and my abs and legs were killing me. *Oh well, no pain, no gain,* I thought and dragged myself back onto the horse.

The rest of the week, we practised more detailed combat riding. These were the kind of stunts you see in films and TV, like how to roll off the horses as if you've been shot or being dragged along the ground by the horse. We did horse boarding too, which is when you stand on a skateboard attached to the back of your horse, and it pulls you along the ground. We also did sword fighting, including rolls and dives on mats, and some aerial hoop and pole work, which I had already been practising for a few years.

Then finally, for the main event, we performed some jousting, which had always been a dream of mine. I used to love watching the knights joust in movies set in the days of King Arthur and had seen jousters at a county fair one year near where I grew up.

Back then, it was all men. But now it was my time to try. Nina set up three targets. You had to ride the horse down one side of the arena, then kick them into gallops, charge up to the targets and knock them over with your jousting sticks. And do you know what? I got them all first time! It was so much fun, like being a kid again, like when I used to climb trees and jump over fences. I finally had my freedom back.

Throughout the training, Nina was so supportive and caring, the total opposite to Toby. She was very complimentary about my skills and gave me loads of positive feedback.

"You're really good," she affirmed. "Stick with it!"

Before I left, I told her what had happened with Toby. She didn't look surprised at all and shook her head.

"There's a real stigma about women in the stunt business," she said with a sigh.

She revealed that when she'd done trick-riding with men, they were always all trying it on with her.

"Unfortunately, you'll get that a lot. Then, if you turn them down, they call you ball busters!" she laughed bitterly. "They either want to sleep with you or try to pull you down."

My heart sank at the thought of having more experiences like the one with Toby or the photographers back in my modelling days.

"So, what do we do?" I asked.

"There's nothing you can do," she declared with a shrug. "You just have to develop a thick skin. Don't listen to them and keep focusing on your own path. You can do it!"

As I drove back to Wrexham, I felt like a new woman. I was alive again. That week with Nina had changed my life again and got me over the barrier of feeling inadequate. Yes, I was a thirty-year-old woman with five kids, but I still had it. *I'm not just a mum,* I thought. *I can still be me!*

A BAD START

When I got home from my week's training, the kids rushed up to give me a big hug. Sure, they'd missed me. But, more than that, they were excited to find out what had happened. I took out my phone and showed them the pictures that Nina had taken of me standing up on the horse and performing all the different tricks. Then I played them a video of me jousting with a lance. I was nervous that they might be worried about me, but they all thought it was brilliant. They loved it so much they wanted to do it themselves.

"Can we go too, Mum?" they yelled, dancing around me as if they were riding horses already. "When will you take us?"

"Soon," I promised and started to make their tea. A mum's work is never done, after all!

I often get asked what it's like, being a single mother to five kids. I'm not going to lie - it's very hard work. But, despite that, it's the best thing in the world and definitely my greatest achievement. Any parent will tell you there's no love greater than that you feel for your children. No one can love you like they do either. No matter how exhausting or annoying they can sometimes be, when they hold you and say, "I'm so happy to have you as my mum," your heart melts. It's just priceless.

Of course I'm biased, but I have to say that my kids are fantastic, each with their own unique personalities. The eldest is Shannon, who was fourteen at the time I started my stunt training. She is very beautiful with long hair and blue eyes; people say she's the spitting image of me but with dark hair. I had changed my hair colour when I was 21 to be blonde. Like her mum, she's obsessed with fitness. She's very acrobatic and can do back flips and aerial skills; she's very flexible too and makes doing the splits look effortless.

Shannon is a nice, bubbly girl but she can be a bit ditzy and gullible – again, just like her mum! One time, I was drinking one of those drinks from Thailand, which has white and black basil seeds. When Shannon saw it, she asked what I was drinking so, for a laugh, I told her frog spawn. Then she rushed out and posted online to all her friends that I was drinking frog sperm! She got a lot of comments about that!

Another time, I was in bed sipping a morning cup of tea, when Shannon ran in with her sister Felicity to ask me a question.

"Mum, do you spit or swallow?" she asked.

"What?" I gasped.

I almost spat out my tea all over the duvet!

"Well, I like to swallow and Fliss likes to spit," Shannon explained.

"Oh my God, what are you on about?" I asked, dreading the answer.

"Toothpaste, of course, Mum!"

Thankfully, they had no idea what I was thinking about!

My next child Malachy is three years younger than Shannon. Mal's a bit stocky, with short brown hair, pale skin and freckles. He's very caring and loving, a real mummy's boy. He'll always help me with his siblings and is so sweet. He's really funny too, with a wicked sense of humour. Once, we were on holiday and he ordered a massive steak. Shannon commented how that was a large meal and asked if he was going to eat all of it.

"Yeah, check out my six-pack," he declared and pulled up his top to show his flabby belly.

My other daughter, Felicity, is three years younger than Mal. She's got long dark hair and freckles, very pretty and stick-thin. Fliss is very clever, with the drive and ambition to succeed, and won a scholarship to go to boarding school. She's also bloody lucky. When we took her to the funfair she won the massive cuddly toy first time and she got first prize in all the competitions at the Anglesey fair, including a foreign holiday for four!

Next up in my big, old brood is Harvey, who's just one year younger than Fliss. He's looks very similar – short dark hair, skinny with freckles – and hugely talented in gymnastics. He was told he could even be on Team GB Gymnastics if he concentrates. But unfortunately, he finds it very hard focus for any length on time because he has severe ADHD. I have to take him for runs every day just to get him out of the house otherwise he starts bouncing off the walls.

Although Harvey can be the biggest pain in the bum you've ever known, he's so funny and cheeky, you can't be angry with him for long. A few years ago, I went to see him in the school play. He was at the front, in the centre, where everyone could see him. I was pulling faces at him and he was copying me; all the parents in the audience could see it. Afterwards, he got told off by the teacher but it was actually my fault so I couldn't really tell him off!

My youngest Blake is three years younger than Harvey, but he's the tiniest thing ever and looks even younger. He was born nine weeks early and is small for his age. He also has dark hair, pale skin and freckles and is very caring. He always tells me how beautiful I am and how much he loves me. What a sweetie!

He can be very cheeky too though; seems it runs in the family. Once I was called into the school because of Blake's "colourful language". He had written a story about Little Red Riding Hood but given the classic tale his own twist.

"She got scared of the wolf," Blake wrote. "So she picked up a saucepan and twatted him over the head with it!"

A comedy writer in the making that one!

Although I was a tomboy in my youth who preferred footballs to dollies, I did always want to have babies. By age sixteen, it was all I could think of. Maybe I was craving that love, even back then. Now I realise that I should have learnt to love myself instead of having the children so young, but I just wanted to be needed. Of course, saying that I wouldn't change a thing at all.

I never thought I'd be a single mother either. Like most girls, growing up, I dreamt that I'd meet a perfect man. I thought I'd find that one person that I'd stay with for life, and we'd be together forever, like my mum and dad. On reflection, I wish I'd been a bit more discerning. If I'd known then what I do now, I would have chosen my baby-fathers more carefully.

I didn't have a good start with men. When I was about twelve, my friends all started getting boyfriends, but I was just the ugly girl the guys would talk to when they wanted to get with my mates.

The first boy that actually fancied me was James Dawson. He was a smart, geeky boy, the same age as me, skinny with glasses and slicked-back hair. For our dates, we used to meet up at the beach. The first time he tried to kiss me, it was so embarrassing. As he went in for a snog, I didn't know what to do, so I kept my mouth shut and he licked my nose and closed lips. Well, that was awkward!

James was a nice guy, but I didn't really fancy him. We hung out over that summer but then we went to different high schools, so I never saw him again. High school really changed me. Because of my developing body, the boys started to take notice. This wasn't always a good thing and even led to more bullying – this time for being attractive!

One girl from high school said that her boyfriend fancied me and ordered me to stay away from him. Of course, I tried but then she saw me outside the petrol station when he was there. It was a total coincidence, but she ran over, grabbed my head and started smashing it into the petrol pump. Then she pushed me to the ground and kicked me in the ribs. Because I was still so scared of the bullies, I never fought back. Eventually, my mum came to get me and even got the police involved so the girl had to pay me damages.

Although my looks were improving, my confidence was still very low. But now I was getting more interest, I had a different boyfriend each week. I didn't do anything with them though, not even kiss, so I ended up being called frigid. It seemed I got bullied whatever I did or didn't do. I couldn't win!

I had a friend called Amy, who had three older brothers. The youngest was a seventeen-year-old called Rob, a good-looking farmer's boy with big muscles. I was fourteen at the time and fell completely in love with him. This was the point that I started to wear make-up and make an effort with my appearance. I still went horse riding, but I gave up playing squash and other tomboyish pastimes. One time, when I was at Amy's house, Rob kissed me and asked me to be his girlfriend. OMG, I couldn't say yes fast enough!

He was very charming and made me feel so special – when he wanted to. I started to hang out with Rob and his group of friends all the time, bad decision on my part. They were a lot older than me and used to take Amy and me joyriding or down the pub, even though there was no way that we looked old enough to drink. These guys were always trying to force me into doing stuff I didn't like. They all did drugs, although luckily, I never did; I didn't even drink or smoke. Once, they were all puffing away, and Rob passed me the joint; I didn't want any, so he blew the smoke in my face. He was trying to get me stoned, probably so I'd go to bed with him, but I just felt sick and went home. That backfired!

Rob's father was a groundsman on an estate, about fifteen miles from my house, and they had a caravan in the middle of the woods. One night, Rob asked me to visit him there. He didn't have a car and I couldn't afford the bus, so I had to walk to the local roundabout and hitchhike. I was only a skinny, little fourteen-year-old, totally stupid and naïve. I didn't give my safety a second thought; I was so in love with Rob. I would have done anything for him.

When I got to Rob's caravan, we started kissing then I lost my virginity to him. To be honest, it was horrible and hurt. But he seemed to enjoy himself and I genuinely thought he really loved me.

Then, at school the next day, Amy didn't talk to me. She told Rob that I was horrible to her or some such teenage rubbish, so he dumped me. It broke my heart. The next night, Amy phoned me to tell me that Rob was already dating another girl, a friend of mine. WTF? I thought we were in love! I couldn't understand it. I was so upset that I puked up my dinner all over the stairs!

After that, I was so depressed about what had happened that I started to become anorexic. I tried to phone Rob, but he wouldn't speak to me. So now I fell back into the pattern of being rejected again. There were other boys that liked me, but I wasn't interested in any of them – only Rob. The pain was too much to take, and I felt like no one understood me. So, although I was only fifteen, I stopped going to school. My parents tried so hard to get me back on the straight and narrow, but I lashed out. I was really moody and wouldn't talk to them anymore. I even locked them out the house, I was so nasty. I took all my pain out on them.

Then, to make matters even worse, my beloved grandfather died. Walter was short and stocky with grey hair and a big laugh, the greatest man ever. He and my gran used to own their own fruit and veg shop. When we visited them in Scotland, I used to help them deliver the newspapers and he would let me put petrol in the car because I was the eldest. I always wanted to please him because he was such fun. He and Granny used to come to our house at Christmas with a big sack of presents and he'd play Santa for us.

Walter loved his food and had a big belly on him. Still, at least he died in the best way ever. He was with my gran at their friends for lunch. Grandad had a massive cream cake then stood up. Granny said he didn't look well, then he collapsed onto the floor and pretty much died instantly. They called the ambulance, but he had already gone.

I was so devastated after my grandfather died. It all happened so quickly. I felt comfortable and safe with Walter, now the bottom had fallen out of my world.

Little did I know, things were about to get even worse. Rob had a best friend called Ed, who was twenty-three years old. One day, he phoned me up.

"Rob wants to meet up with you," Ed declared.

"Really?" I gushed. "That's fantastic!"

I hadn't spoken to Rob for about four weeks by this point, but I was still madly in love with him. *Maybe things will be different now,* I thought. *Maybe he does really love me.*

The emotions were overwhelming. I felt that my life was complete again. I got changed into a pretty vest top and leggings. I couldn't tell my parents where I was going so I snuck out of the house. As usual, I didn't have the money for the bus, so I had to hitchhike. I walked to the roundabout, stuck out my thumb, and got a lift from a lorry driver straight away. I didn't think about any risks; all I could think of was seeing my gorgeous Rob again!

Ed told me to meet Rob in the middle of the woods. The lorry driver dropped me off at the side of the road and I walked across the bypass to get to the land. When I saw the car sitting there, my heart sang. I was ecstatic that Rob wanted to see me again.

But, as I got closer, I saw that it was just Ed in the car. *WTF?*

"Where's Rob?" I snapped.

"Don't worry, he's just up there," Ed replied. "Come on, let's walk together."

So we marched up the hill until we reached a ditch.

"Let's sit here a minute," Ed suggested.

"But I want to see Rob," I moaned.

But Ed was insistent.

"Relax, he's coming. We can wait for him here."

Reluctantly, I sat down next to Ed. This was so annoying. When was my true love going to arrive?

Then Ed turned towards me with a lecherous smile.

"I've always found you attractive."

"Sorry, but I just like Rob," I told him.

But then he leaned over and pushed his tongue into my mouth.

"Stop that," I shouted.

"Give me a kiss," he demanded.

"No!"

I wouldn't kiss him, so Ed shoved me to the ground. He pushed my face into the dirt so I couldn't shout, then held me down. He undid my top and grabbed my boobs, then pulled down my leggings and raped me.

When Ed had finished, he rolled off me. He threw the money at me for the bus home and told me to go.

"But if you ever tell anyone about this, I'm going to find you and fucking kill you," he screamed.

I was absolutely petrified. I pulled up my clothes, scrambled to my feet and ran away.

RUNNING AWAY

I was shaking as I sat on the bus home, replaying the events in my mind. As soon as I arrived, I locked myself in my room. I felt all alone and like I didn't belong anywhere. *There's no one out there that cares for me or even likes me,* I thought. I wondered if what had happened with Ed was my fault. *Maybe I made him do this to me?* I felt dirty and humiliated. I went from being on such a high at the idea of being reunited with Rob to crashing down into this pit of hell.

I felt scared and worried that Ed would do it again. I didn't know what to do so I phoned a friend; I didn't feel that I could tell my parents. After I told her what had happened, my friend told me to come out with her and try to forget it. So I went to Lowestoft where she introduced me to the twenty-year-old guy from Norfolk that she was dating, and his flatmate Matthew. Over the next couple of weeks, I started to date Matthew. Then, one day, I went to see him in Norfolk and moved in with him and his friend.

I didn't really fancy Matthew, but I had nowhere else to go. I don't know what got into my head, but I just couldn't go home. My parents were completely shocked; my mum guessed that something had happened, but I wouldn't tell her the truth. I didn't even go and get my stuff; my mum just bagged up all my belongings and put them in the garage. My parents went to the police to try to get me to come back, but I was just turning sixteen, so there was nothing they could do. I was a grown-up now.

Matthew was a nice guy and very sweet to me, but he didn't have any ambition or drive. He and his mate worked in a Bernard Matthews chicken factory and lived in a hideous, run-down flat. Downstairs there was a fishing shop; you could actually see the fishing tackle through the holes in the wooden floor and the whole place stank of fish and maggots. The place was so dirty, you'd wipe your feet on the way out and not on the way in!

But at least it was far away from Ed, Rob and the bullies from school. That's all I cared about for now. We were all so poor, we only just got by. Once there was no electricity for two days, so we had to cook by holding a saucepan above some candles for hours just to heat it up. Matthew and his friend used to go and nick food from supermarkets but, because of my Christian background, I would never steal.

I was in an awful state, but I couldn't see any way out. Then, one day, I was in the local supermarket. On the noticeboard, they had a leaflet for the local amateur dramatics group, the Swaffham Players. I went along to the meeting and they were rehearsing for a production of *South Pacific*. The leading lady was lovely; she was in her forties and had a great voice. *If I stick with this lot, I can be like her one day*, I thought. They gave me a small role singing and dancing in the chorus and I started to rehearse every week. The buzz of being on stage made me feel giddy with excitement and people said that they enjoyed watching me perform.

At the same time, I got a job working behind the bar. I was only 16 so I lied about my age because the only jobs going were in pubs. Fortunately, they didn't ask for ID in those days. However, not long after I started working there, a group of men came to rent rooms at the pub. After my shift, they tried to get me to come upstairs with them. I told them I wasn't that kind of girl. But one night, I was about to leave out of the back door of the pub so that they wouldn't see me, when one of the guys followed me out.

He tried to get me to come upstairs but I didn't want to, so he pressed me against the wall. There was no way I wanted a replay of the situation with Ed, so I kicked him hard on the leg and ran away. I could hear the boss shouting after me, but I didn't look back. I thought I had got away from the situation. But when I went into work the next day, the manager was horrible to me. At the end of the shift, he told me I was fired for sleeping with a customer; to get back at me for rejecting him, the guy had told them that I had gone up to his room. Because I had left through the back door, my boss had believed him.

Not having a job, I was now even more vulnerable. But I didn't want to go back home and couldn't face seeing my friends or family. In the daytime, I used to just walk around the town and try to figure out how to get away. I was feeling so down. The boyfriend I was living with was okay, but our relationship wasn't going anywhere. When I came home in the evening, we wouldn't talk, but just went to sleep, sometimes without saying a word.

Fortunately, I was still in the Swaffham Players, so I buried my head in the sand and concentrated on the show. I immersed myself in the world of *South Pacific* – much better than Norfolk! Some of the other actors were nice, but I never opened up about anything that had happened to me. Deep down, I still felt so betrayed. It seemed like everyone was constantly out to get me and no one liked me, no matter what I did. I was really depressed but acting helped because it took me out of myself. Drama was my only escape.

There were three people in the cast about my age but mainly they were quite a bit older. One guy was called Justin, a thirty-year old pig farmer, the joker of the group. Everyone liked him because he was so funny and good on stage. One night after rehearsal, Justin offered to drive me home. I felt comfortable with him because he had a strong resemblance to my grandad Walter, the same height, chubby body and funny personality.

As we got chatting, Justin told me that I was very talented, and offered to help me achieve my goals. As the show date approached, we were rehearsing five times a week and Justin and I got closer. He made me laugh and feel more hopeful. We would constantly talk about my future. He told me I could do anything and made me feel like I could make it. Justin filled the void in my life left by my grandfather's death. I didn't fancy him at all, but I saw him as a father figure, someone who could protect me. He had his own house and would buy me food and make me feel safe. How it got romantic, I don't know. But one night we went for dinner and ended up going back to his place. I didn't want to have sex with him, but it just sort of happened. I almost felt that I had to in return for the kindness he had shown me.

But, when we were in bed that first time, it was weird. It felt familiar but wrong. *What am I doing?* I thought. *He reminds me of my grandad.* I think he was embarrassed too, because I was so much younger than him. But that didn't stop him, of course. Just one month later, I moved in with Justin. Anything seemed better than staying at that filthy flat that stunk of fish. I just left everything I had there, which wasn't much. I didn't even tell my other boyfriend that I was leaving. I still feel bad about that now.

I had only been at Justin's place for a month when 9/11 happened, the event that rocked the world. I was watching the news constantly, in panic mode. During every single advert break in-between the news, a pregnancy test advert came up. *It's a sign,* I thought, *Maybe I'm pregnant.* I went to the chemist and got a test. As I weed on the stick, I was shaking. Then I saw the fateful two lines appear. I was only sixteen and still felt like a child myself, but, like it or not, baby number one was on its way.

TRAINING

When I came back after my first trick riding course with Nina, I was high for a whole month. It was such a relief that the kids were happy for me and supportive. Now I was home I knew I had to seize the bull by its horns and keep up the momentum. First things first, I needed to get another job and keep the money coming in – all this training didn't come cheap.

I soon got work cleaning local people's houses. I've always been an OCD clean freak and I don't have any snobbery about jobs so I can just get on and do whatever it takes. Now I had my income sorted, I thought about what other sports I could practise locally to help me improve my trick riding. I checked the British Stunt Register and Group B or "Falling" included Gymnastics, which seemed like the perfect place to start.

Researching online, I found a gymnastics studio just up the road from where I lived – funny how you never notice these things until you start looking for them. So I signed up for gymnastics class every Monday night. Turns out, there were three other lads taking the classes who were doing the stunt register too. One guy Jack was a world champion kick boxer and one of the best throwers I've ever met; he just annihilates his opponent in every fight he has. He's also very funny and we hit it off straight away. We are still close – everyone thinks we're brother and sister. He is my ultimate BMF (best male friend), and I trust him with my life.

I loved those Monday night classes with the guys. The back flips were particularly hilarious because I was completely hopeless at them. Every time I attempted it, I would fall on my head. We'd have a good giggle about it then I'd get up and try again. That's what Jack said he oves about me; the drive I have to keep trying and the ability to laugh at myself and my mistakes.

They say you have to do something over one hundred times to remember it. I made sure I learnt one move each week then I'd practise it every day. I'd do acrobatics with the kids at home too. They loved it when I'd put them on my feet and twiddle them in the air or we'd all do handstands together. The children got really into gymnastics, and they were brilliant, especially Harvey who could do triple flips and everything. It was a great way of spending quality family time too and keep them away from the TV.

I also started basic riding again at my local stables. I loved being back on a horse – one of my favourite places in the world. But my body didn't like it so much; when I woke up the next morning, my back was in bits. I realised that I was going to have to build up my strength and be careful that I didn't try too much too quickly and do myself an injury. In order to keep myself on track, I set myself challenges. I found that, if I set goals and mapped out a schedule, I would make good progress. You can achieve anything like that. At the time, I had a friend called Sally who was performing burlesque. I went to see her show and she was brilliant. After the show, we went for a drink and Sally asked if I wanted to do burlesque too. That was certainly another challenge, but of course I said yes. I love to dance, which is a great way to express yourself, and could always wiggle my hips with style!

To start with, I tried pole dancing. I've always liked it as an art form; it looks so elegant and the upper body strength you get from it is amazing. So I put a pole in my room and started to practise every day. Before long, I could do all the moves like the classic position *The Flag,* when you are vertical to the pole and hold your whole bodyweight in a straight line at ninety degrees. It's really hard on the arms and God, it aches your core, but it looks great!

You can do what you want in burlesque, so I decided not to do the traditional routine with the nipple tassels. Instead, I did my own style where I would just strip down to a bra and a thong then do a dance routine with flips, jumps and acrobatics. I even did a shoulder stand on the chair and held up my whole body weight. It was quite athletic really and made me ache as much as horse riding!

My first public performance was in a club with Sally and another girl. It went brilliantly and was so exciting. Then Sally asked me if wanted to perform in another show on my own. Of course, I agreed - then wondered what on earth I was going to do for my act. I saw a girl online who set a hoop on fire then danced around with it like a flaming Goddess. Wow, that was cool! I had hula hooped a bit in my youth but didn't really know anything about it. But how hard could it be?!

In the back of my mind, I thought it could be an extra unusual skill that I could use on a film set if I ever needed to. So I gave myself twenty-eight days to learn fire hula hoop. The first time I set it alight my ponytail got stuck in the hoop and it singed the back of my hair. But, after the initial shock, I just gave my hair a trim and got back to practising again – although I tied my hair up in a bun from then on!

Around the same time, I was single and thinking about getting out there and dating again. My friend Karen came around one night. We had a few Proseccos and when she heard about my plan to find a new guy, she told me to go on *Plenty of Fish*. So I downloaded the dating app and had a look. Oh my God, it was awful. You can't believe the amount of dick picks I got sent! Do men really think that's going to work?

However, one guy seemed nice so I thought, I might as well give it a try. After all my problems with men, I had lost my confidence in dating. It felt very scary, but Karen convinced me to go through with it – I had to get back on the horse sometime! So I messaged this guy and we got chatting. After a few days, he asked to take me out. Although there wasn't really the initial attraction there, he was a lovely guy, so I thought, *Why not?* We met up and had a lovely dinner in a fancy restaurant. I didn't really tell him how bad my past experiences with men were. I just said I'd had a couple of dickheads, as you do!

We decided to meet up for a second date. *Maybe the attraction will grow*, I thought. So he came round my house one evening when the children were in bed. I had been practising all day with the fire hoop for my burlesque show. I was really excited because I was trying a new move which was risky and quite unusual. When he arrived, the guy

44

was quite nervous so I could tell that he really liked me. I explained all about the show that I was rehearsing for.

"Check out this new move I've got," I announced. "Can you film it for me?"

It always helped me to look back at my moves on camera to see how I could improve.

"Of course," he replied and took out his phone.

The guy sat on the edge of the sofa, a mix of terror and excitement on his face. I lay on my back and put my leg up in the air then flicked the fire hoop onto my foot. I started the move; it was going really well, and he was loving it. But then the hoop slid off my leg and whacked him hard in the face, right between the eyes. It gave him a proper bruise. Luckily the hoop wasn't on fire at the time!

The guy caught the whole thing on film – we should have sent it into Britain's Funniest Home Videos! Fortunately, he just laughed about it, but I was so embarrassed, I didn't meet up with him again. I met another guy on the dating app. His name was Lincoln and he was genuinely sweet. He worked in the stock market in London and was very well off. He even drove around in a Ferrari.

We went on a few dates and everything went well until it got to the stage when it was time to take things further. Well, I'd better make an impression, I thought. So I got all dressed up in a basque and suspenders, which he seemed to like. Then he asked me to talk dirty to him. I didn't know what to say to that. I wracked my brains, but this was the best I could come up with.

"Leave the lights on," I whispered. "I like to see who I'm having sex with."

"What?" he responded.

I paused – I really didn't know how to reply.

"Let's just leave the dirty talk," he said. "It's probably not your strong point."

I agreed and decided to focus more on my strengths. I put on some sexy music and started to do an erotic dance. He was getting very turned on. But then I turned around, fell over and bashed my head into a wall! I didn't see him again either.

So much for the dating app. I decided to go through the traditional route and meet people in real life. Once, when I was in Spain for a filming job, and I met a guy out there. He seemed nice so we went out for dinner then he came back to my apartment. We were sitting having a drink when he decided to kiss me. We had a good old snog, but then, from the corner of my eye, I noticed that the sofa was on fire. As he'd leaned in to make his move, he'd pushed the cushions back and they were too close to the gas heater.

When I saw the flames, I jumped up and screamed. We had to drag the sofa out of the patio doors and throw it on the pool, along with all the cushions. I didn't date the guy again, but at least we had a sense of humour. He said it was the hottest date he'd ever had! There was another guy that I got to know through mutual friends. We didn't ever go on a date, but we used to hang out at the gym and do fitness stuff together. He wanted to take it further but I said no as he was only nineteen years old and I was thirty with five kids!

But sadly, this guy wouldn't take no for an answer. He started to get obsessed and stalk me. He'd come around my house and sit outside my door at ten at night. In the end, I had to call the police. Fortunately, they put an end to it, and I didn't hear from him again. That put me off dating; my kids come first and I wouldn't do anything that would endanger them in any way.

I felt nervous to be putting myself out there again anyway. I don't think I was really ready emotionally, but I felt like I should push myself to try to move on. For some misguided reason, I thought dating would fix this problem. It was as if I was seeing other men to find out who I was. Big mistake.

But after these few experiences, I knew it wasn't the right time. My best friends agreed, the ones that really knew me.

"Give it a few years and you'll be well ahead of yourself," they said.

And they were right.

So I decided to stick to getting on one kind of horse only - for the time being at least. As soon as I had saved up enough money, I went back to Hereford for another training week. It had been six months since I was last there and Nina was amazed by how much I had progressed. All those back flips falling on my head must have done

46

something. The gymnastics helped me get my core muscles engaged because when you ride at speed, you really need to engage your core strength, or you're stuck. I've had five kids too, so I really had to work at it.

Instead of walking and trotting, we went straight into doing the cantering. We also did the handstands on the horse, while it's galloping. We practised the same tricks that I had done in our first training but this time at a much higher speed and over a greater distance. Then I learnt a new stunt – the Death Hang. This is when you gallop on a horse that's going at a speed of up to thirty miles an hour and you dangle off by one leg. You have to be very precise; you've only got a couple of seconds to get into the trick and five seconds in the hang. Then you have to pull the reins up quickly to make sure you're out of the stunt so you can stop the horse crashing into barrier at the end.

My horse was an incredible chestnut cross Arab called Sunny. He was very sensitive and could sense that I was nervous so although he had to gallop, he started off slowly.

"He was working with you there," Nina said afterwards, and I felt that she was right.

So we did the Death Hang again – this time at the proper speed. I managed to get into the trick okay but this time I had a costume failure. I was wearing a vest top and when I went into the hang, my left breast fell out! Nina and I burst out laughing, which almost made me mess up the stunt, but I managed to get back up and put my boob away just in time.

All week we carried on with all the stunts, getting into bigger and better tricks. We even doubled up and did some tricks together. All this was just practising in the barn though. After three days, Nina told me,

"It's all well and good doing tricks in a circle but when you are out there on the field, it's another matter."

So that afternoon, she took me out onto a long strip of ground where you can gallop and really pick up speed.

There are so many things that can go wrong when you're doing stunts like the Death Hang. You might not connect properly and bounce off the horse and fall on the floor. Or, if you get caught in the stirrup as you're doing the trick, when you go under the horse, you might hit the horse's feet. There's also the danger of getting stuck in a trick and not being able to pull yourself up in time to get out of the way. If you aren't properly prepared, you can fall off the horse at great speed and easily die. Once the trick is under way, there is no time to think. You have to know what you are doing. I think that's why you learn so quickly with stunts – if you don't focus, you could be dead. That certainly helps focus the mind!

However, the strange thing was, although I knew all these potential pitfalls, I didn't feel scared. I don't know if it was just the adrenalin, but I knew I could do it. It felt like I had waited for this moment all my life. For some reason, I believed in myself. And just as well because if you don't have the belief, you could be in serious trouble. Lots of women complain that they have that sense of losing themselves after they become a mum but doing all this stunt work enabled me to find myself again. It helped me be happy, carefree and love life. It was amazing how much I changed in such a short space of time when I really decided to take action and turn my life around.

I vowed to go back to Nina whenever I had the money and aimed for once a month. But even back home, doing the gymnastics and burlesque, I was so excited and motivated. The kids and I had lots of family time too. To keep my cardio up we'd do lots of walks and trekking in the local mountains, which they all loved. We became closer as a family and more connected.

Because I was in the right frame of mind, I was happy and positive, so I could be a better mum too. I was there for them, they had all my attention, as did my friends. I didn't have a boyfriend but, for the first time in my life, I didn't need one. I was happy and complete on my own.

TRAPPED

I wish I had felt that self-love at sixteen. Unfortunately, my traumatic childhood experiences and crippling insecurity had led me into Justin's arms who turned out to be yet another unsuitable man. And now, after just one month together, I was going to have his baby!

After the test showed as positive, I just sat in silence, staring at the wall. *What the hell am I going to do now?* When Justin got in from work, I told him the big news. He wasn't impressed. He was angry that I was ruining his life and trapping him with a kid, even though it was by no means done on purpose. Afterwards, we didn't speak for a while. I knew that I didn't want a child with Justin but, being Catholic, an abortion was out of the question, so I had no choice.

In my teenage years, when my mum was upset with me for being a rebel, hanging out with boys, not caring enough about my education or running away from home she used to always say the same thing.

"If you're not careful, you're going to be pregnant by the time you're sixteen. You'll do nothing with your life and end up having kids."

I used to protest at the time but now I had gone and proved her right. Although I was speaking to my parents now, we weren't close in the slightest. I still couldn't open up about what had really happened to me back home and the difficult turn my life had taken since.

When I finally plucked up the courage to tell my mum the news, she went mental. No surprise there!

"I knew this would happen," she yelled. "I told you that you'd waste your life and get pregnant. I don't want anything to do with it, you'll have to stick with Justin."

She was furious. So was my dad. However, about three months later, they finally agreed to come up and see me. I'd just had the first scan – at first, when I showed Mum the picture, she wasn't interested, but eventually she came around to the idea. Throughout my pregnancy, she supported me and helped me buy stuff for the baby. She came up a few times and asked to be there for the birth. Although she was very disappointed, she did want to be there for her daughter.

While I was pregnant, Justin got a job on a farm in Hertfordshire. He sold his house to pay off his considerable debts and we moved into the three-bedroom house that he got with the job. But although Justin had slowly come around to the fact that we were having a baby, his parents were horrible. They were quite stuck up with lots of money and a big house, very lord and lady of the manor!

When I told Justin's mother that I was pregnant, she dismissed it at first.

"It must be someone else's. It's not my son's."

She wasn't happy about it at all.

"It's a disgrace. I can't tell my friends about this," she complained. "How can you have a baby? You're only a child yourself."

I couldn't really argue with that. I felt like everyone was judging me for having a kid at my age. When I went into hospital, even the midwives were rude to me. Justin was with me at the birth, along with my mum. I was a couple of days late and very uncomfortable, so I was induced. It was so embarrassing because the student doctor that examined me wasn't much older than me. I was only seventeen and having all these doctors and nurses peering into your bits was very daunting.

Still denying the parentage, Justin's folks wouldn't have anything to do with me until I'd had the baby. Immediately afterwards, they marched me to a clinic to do a DNA test. I knew 100% that it was definitely Justin's; there weren't any other men around and Shannon looks exactly like him. The moment they knew it was Justin's, his parents wanted to see the baby and be sent lots of pictures so at least they came around too.

Although it was quite overwhelming, I loved having a baby. Now I had something that I could care for, that was really mine. However, before long, it triggered all my insecurities and I started to feel quite terrible.

"You can't handle being a mum," I'd berate myself. "You're going to be hopeless."

I was getting depressed on my own, so I joined a baby club. Because I was so young, none of the other mums would talk to me. However, I did make one friend called Tracey. She was thirty and had an older daughter as well as her new baby. She lived just down the road and really took the time to help me. We'd walk the kids in the buggies, and she'd take me shopping every day. She told me not to buy processed baby food but showed me how to make fresh food and look after the baby. She was like a mother to me, which was exactly what I needed at the time.

Although we were living at the farm, Justin and I never spent much time together; he was always at work, whilst I was at home with the littlun. On the rare occasions that we went out together, he wouldn't hold my hand because I looked so young that people thought he was my father. He didn't help with Shannon at all. I knew that he didn't really want to be with me either. He was still in love with his first girlfriend that had dumped him. He would talk about her whenever we went to the places that they used to go to together.

This went on for a few months then Justin got a job in America. He did artificial semination and was quite high up in the pig farming industry; he was very clever and always worked hard. We left Shannon with my parents and went over to Virginia for a week to see if we liked it. When we arrived at the hotel, there was a problem with the booking and Justin started to have a go at me about it in public. Afterwards, the manager came over to me, a nice guy in his thirties. He looked at me then looked at Justin.

"What's he like?" he muttered. "Is that your pimp?"

I thought it was a joke at first. But then I realised that he was serious.

"No, it's my partner," I explained.

The manager looked shocked - he didn't believe it in the slightest.

"You're beautiful, why are you with him?" he balked. "Look in that mirror then look at him. He's much older than you and so rude to you."

He just didn't get it at all.

Despite everything, Justin and I had a great week. I really liked America, so we decided to move there. Maybe this would be a new start for our family. I didn't really love Justin, but now we had a child I felt that it was right to stick with him, in the Catholic way.

My parents tried to persuade me not to stay with him. My dad even said, "I don't care about religion. I'll give you the money now if you take Shannon and go away."

I was so shocked that my dad could say this. I looked over at mum and she nodded too. Deep down, I knew they were right. I felt myself that I shouldn't really be with him, but I didn't have the guts to leave.

I was still young and immature and couldn't see anything changing. Even Justin's parents were against us. I could have read all these signs and got away but I was resigned to the fact that this would be my life. The universe, however, had other plans.

THE CRASH

The job in America fell through so Justin and I stayed at the farm – and the disappointment seemed to change him. When he came in after work, he was always tired. He wouldn't have a shower and would just sit in the chair having been on the pig farm all day. Then he'd turn on the TV and look at porn in front of me – he watched it a lot. After grinning at the screen, he would turn to me and look me up and down with contempt.

"You're ugly and fat," he'd sneer. "No one will ever want you."

It made me feel hideous again, just like at school.

What had happened to the funny man that I met at the drama society who was always praising me and encouraging me to follow my dreams? Now Justin never listened to me and didn't believe anything I said. We argued all the time; especially if I ever wanted to go out or have friends round. Once we had a massive row and he threw the used cat litter tray over me.

He was mentally very hard work and tired me out with his behaviour. By now he had becoming very possessive and controlling. He kept telling me what I could and couldn't do, where I should and shouldn't go, who I could and couldn't speak to. He even started to lock me in the house so I couldn't leave without him.

Justin told me that I was mad and even tried to convince my friends that they were stupid for talking to me. He tried to make Tracey believe I was this crazy teenager who was out of control and off her rocker.

"Can't you see that she's manipulative?" he told her.

But Tracey always had my back.

"No, she's just a kid. You're a 33-year-old man," Tracey reminded him. "You should be behaving like a mature adult."

She could see that he was trying to manipulate me. She used to suggest that I leave but I couldn't do it. So once again, I was in a position of being vulnerable and bullied, just like through my childhood. It was as if, because I had experienced so much of this already, I kept drawing more of it to myself. I couldn't believe that I had ended up in this position but didn't know how to get out of it.

In the end, I decided to go back to work. At least that would get me out of the house a bit; earning my own money would give me some independence and I could pay for driving lessons. I got a job in a petrol station. I was running it all myself and had quite a lot of responsibility, which helped to build up my confidence. I started to feel that I wasn't completely useless after all.

After a few months of working, I passed my driving test and my dad gave me a car. That Christmas, I even drove to my parents on my own with Shannon. Justin could see me getting stronger and more independent, which he hated. By now, we both knew it was over, but we were still together – just. I felt like I was going under. I knew I had to do something to claw back my life. Then fate played a helping hand.

I saw an advert in the local papers for an amateur dramatic group in Stotfold. I started to go to classes there one evening a week, acting and singing. I really enjoyed it, everyone was so friendly and complimentary about my performing. Some people from the acting group ran a karaoke night at the pub at the weekends and asked me to help them with it, for which they would pay me. They liked my energy and the way I could get a crowd going. They even commented on how confident I appeared, which was bizarre considering how I felt inside.

That night was to be my first gig with the karaoke group. It had caused a lot of arguments as Justin wanted me to stay in the house, but I wouldn't. I think he sensed that I would soon be gone. I had been at my parents' house that week with Shannon, and I was driving home to Stotfold. Shannon was strapped in the back, and I was feeling excited about how I was mobile now so I could do what I liked.

I was driving about seventy miles an hour on a straight road. Suddenly, a little, white Clio came whizzing around the corner on the wrong side of the road and smashed into me then flipped over on its roof.

My blue Vauxhall Astra skidded off the road and spun around in the field next to the road. I remember it in slow motion. *This is it, I'm going to die*, I thought. My car was whirling, I couldn't breathe, and I couldn't hear anything from Shannon. *Is my poor baby alive?* Then the car stopped and Shannon screamed. *Thank God*, I thought, *she's okay*. Now I knew that she would live, I looked up at the sky and surrendered. *That's it, I can die now.*

Then, all of a sudden, it was as if someone smacked me on the back and I started breathing again. It was so surreal, the sort of thing that you imagine only happens to other people and not to you. I came to and realised that I was in the field. I looked down at my feet. The crash happened so fast; I had put my foot over the break but didn't have time to press it. Where the Clio hit me on my right side, my foot was all mangled in the clutch. *Shit, I can't get out*, I thought. *What am I going to do?* There was so much smoke pouring out of the engine. I prayed that the car wouldn't burst into flames.

Now I became aware of all the people crowding around me. I started to panic that the car might be on fire, so I screamed at them to get my daughter out. A man pulled Shannon out of her baby seat in the back, and luckily, she only had a bump on her head. Then I asked them to get me out of the car. They had to pull me out because my foot was stuck, but they managed to drag me out of the passenger side.

Fortunately, there was no damage to the car behind and all the people were very kind. Not long after, the ambulance came. I was dazed, drifting in and out of consciousness, but I just about managed to tell them what had happened and give them my mum's number. When we got to the hospital, the doctors checked Shannon over and thankfully, she was fine. Then the doctors checked me and said that my major organs had a massive swelling around them. My foot was very swollen too, but it wasn't broken. My parents arrived at the hospital in a total panic. Mum said that she'd had a bad feeling about something just after I left.

I had to stay in hospital for about three weeks. Mum took time off work to stay at my house and look after Shannon then bring her to the hospital, which was thirty minutes' drive away. They came in every day without fail. Justin only came in twice the whole time! When I came out of hospital, I felt very emotional. It was as if I needed those three weeks to seriously consider what I was doing with my life. *I deserve better than this*, I thought. *Something has to change.*

I was on crutches, so my mum picked me up from hospital and drove me back to the farm. I was crying the whole way home. When I arrived back at the house, Justin was out, and the place was in a terrible state. Like I said, I'm an OCD clean freak so, even though I'd just come out of hospital, I started clearing up.

As I tidied the bedroom, I found a used condom.

"Where did this come from?" I blurted.

"I don't know," Mum replied. "Where did you find it?"

"By the bed."

"Well, that's definitely not mine. Me and your dad are past that age. We don't need them anymore."

I knew this could only mean one thing – it was Justin's. I didn't want to speak to him, I was too upset. Mum put me in the car and took me back to her house. Later, Justin phoned and asked where I was and when I would return.

"I'm not coming back," I declared and told him about finding the condom.

"It wasn't me," Justin whined.

Predictably, he blamed it on my parents, and started to yell.

"You're a whore, you've planted it there. Any excuse to get away."

It was total abuse. In the end, my mum said, "You don't have to take this," and I hung up. When my mum told my dad what had happened and how Justin tried to put the blame on him, Dad just laughed. He couldn't believe it. Afterwards, Justin started phoning Tracey and all my other my friends, telling them they were so thick that they can't see through my lies and deceit. But they realised that he was just making up more stories.

So that was the end of my chapter with Justin. At last, I had finally got away and could concentrate on looking after my daughter and getting on with the rest of my life. It felt amazing to be away from Justin. It was as if the universe conspired to make me have that car crash and stop me going back to him. I felt like some unknown force was guiding me and my life. I knew that I was destined for bigger things.

GUIDANCE

They say when the student is ready, the teacher will appear. I've been very lucky to meet lots of amazing people along the way who have inspired me and given me guidance at the perfect moment. Of course, there are some right so and so's in this industry, but there are some wonderfully supportive and generous folk too.

After my second horse riding week with Nina, I knew life was about to get hectic with all the training and work. So before everything got too busy, I decided to go on a holiday to Mallorca, just me and the children. I knew I needed to spend some quality time with them and give them my full attention. I always wanted them to feel that they were the most important thing for me.

After the flight, we took a taxi to the hotel, which was beautiful, with a huge pool. As we were checking in, I saw a couple of famous people in the lobby. There was an American singer and actress who had come to Malaga to do a concert and a British actor in his fifties who I recognised because he used to star in TV's *The Bill*. *That's a good sign,* I thought and prayed that I'd get the chance to speak to them in person.

The kids were so excited to be on holiday. As soon as we had dropped off the bags in our room, they wanted to run down to the pool straight away. So we went downstairs and sprawled out on the sun loungers. I lay back and felt the hot Spanish sun on my face – this was the life. Then suddenly, who should appear but the actor that I saw earlier. He sat down on a lounger just a couple of meters from me. I decided that this was another sign; I had to go and talk to him. Although I can be shy, I know that when life opens a door for you, you have to be brave and jump through.

I took a deep breath and went to say hello, revealing that I recognised him from the TV.

"I hope you don't mind me talking to you," I added, giving him the chance to get rid of me if he wasn't in the mood to talk to a stranger.

"Of course not," he said with a smile. "Take a seat."

So I sat down and we discussed all the shows that he had been in and his favourite roles that he'd played. I loved hearing all his showbiz stories. It was like a sneaky peek behind the curtain into what life was really like as a jobbing actor.

Then he asked me what I did for a living. I told him I was training to be a stunt woman and would love to become an actress too.

"It's my dream job," I revealed, "and all I've ever wanted to do."

"Then you should go for it!" he replied.

He was very positive and encouraging; he didn't moan about how difficult the profession was or try to put me off. He told me that I had great energy and a good look for the business.

Then the actor gave me some practical advice on how to go about getting into the industry. He told me to read some particular books on acting and go to drama classes then put together a showreel. I could then send that to directors and producers so they could see how I came across on camera. He even gave me the names of some agents and casting directors to send my showreel to. This guy was on holiday, so he didn't have to advise me, but he spent half an hour running through it all. What a dude!

I looked over at the children to check all was okay, but they were still happily playing by the sun lounger.

"Are they your kids?" the actor asked.

"Yup," I replied. "All five of them!"

When the actor found out that I was a single mother to five children, it blew him away.

"Wow, you're a big family," he laughed. "You should go more public with the kids, get them on social media. People would love it!"

I thanked him for his advice and said I'd think about it. However, at the time, I wasn't sure if I wanted to do that. Apart from the odd scroll through Facebook, I had been so busy bringing up my family that I hadn't really got into social media. Plus, I felt protective of my children and was nervous about putting them in the public eye.

Right, it was time to let the actor get on with his sunbathing now; he was on holiday after all. I said goodbye and went back to the kids. They asked me who I had been talking to for so long and I revealed that he was a famous actor.

"I want to be just like him," I exclaimed. "And now I know what I need to do next."

They were super excited for me and gave me a big kiss.

Then I realised that 9-year-old Harvey wasn't in the immediate area.

"Where's your brother?" I asked Shannon, but she just shrugged.

I looked over and saw that Harvey was over the other side of the pool. A woman was sunbathing topless, so cheeky little Harv had pinched her bikini top from the side of her lounger. Now the woman was looking everywhere for it, whilst my naughty son had put it on top of his head and was running around the pool, laughing.

"Oi, Harvey," I shouted. "Give that back!"

With a sheepish grin, Harvey gave the bikini top back to the woman and apologised. Fortunately, he's so adorable that she just laughed.

It was midday by now and baking hot.

"Can we go in the pool now?" the kids begged.

They had all put their costumes on by themselves.

"Of course," I replied. "Let me just get changed then I'll come in the shallow end with you."

There were no lifeguards there, so you had to keep an eye on the little ones yourself.

I turned to get my bikini but before I knew it, my littlest Blake ran up and jumped into the deep end of the pool. He was only six and not a confident swimmer. He panicked and started coughing and spluttering. I had no time to think. I just ran over and jumped in the water to save him. I was fully clothed and even still wearing my shoes!

Everyone around the pool was watching and they burst out laughing. As I carried Blake out of the pool, they cheered. I was so embarrassed. But in the end, I saw the funny side. So did the actor, who had been watching all this too.

As I dried off Blake, he came over to us.

"You guys are hilarious," he exclaimed, chuckling. "You really should record what you're doing and get it up on social media. You'll all be stars!"

As he said goodbye and left, I thought about his words. Little did I know how prophetic they would be.

For the rest of the week, we had a lovely family holiday. It wasn't without accidents though – with five young kids, it never is. One day, I was in the lobby whilst the kids were all out the front of the hotel, running around and playing tag. Suddenly, Shannon rushed in screaming.

"Felicity's fallen down a hole!"

"What?" I gasped.

I ran out to see what had happened. Outside the hotel, there was a big sewage pipe. It was covered up by leaves but, you know what kids are like, they get in everywhere. Poor Flic had fallen into the pipe and was covered in shit!

I leant down and managed to pull her out, thank God. We were lucky we didn't lose her completely; if she had gone all the way in, she would have died. What a way to go! We bought Felicity back into the hotel room and washed her. Fortunately, she was okay about it all and quite calm. She was more grossed out that she was in sewage up to her neck than anything else!

Ah, the joys of parenthood. But to be honest, I'm so clumsy, I can be like a big kid myself sometimes. On our last day in Spain, we went on a boat trip to a stunning part of the coast that you could only reach by sea. We all jumped in the water and splashed around having fun.

As the boat was getting ready to leave, I wanted to jump in one more time.

"Be careful," Harvey yelled. "There's a jelly fish!"

I hate jelly fish, but I couldn't see any, so I thought Harv was just winding me up – as usual.

But then, as I dived in the water, all the kids started screaming with him.

"Jelly fish! Jelly fish!"

I looked around to try and see it and ended up head butting the jelly fish and it stuck to my face. OMG, how vile! The kids were howling with laughter. Fortunately, I had goggles on, but I still had this pink jelly fish stuck to my face.

"How do I get it off?" I cried. "If I touch it, it's going to sting me."

But the kids were laughing so much they couldn't speak.

"Thanks for your help, guys!" I groaned. "Guess I'll just sort it out myself."

In the end, I put my head under the water and thrashed about until, eventually, it fell off. I was very lucky that it didn't sting me, and I didn't end up with a massive lump on my face. It took me a bit longer to see the funny side of that one, although, of course, I did in the end. Shame we didn't get that one on film!

We got back from the holiday in one piece – just about. Feeling refreshed, I decided to follow up on the information that the actor had given me. I still wanted to do stunt work, but I longed to start acting too. I began reading a lot of books on the subject. I studied Stanislavsky, Brecht, and Stella Adler, who was Marlon Brando's "Method Acting" teacher. I even read books by all sorts of performers and theatre people and even some on script writing and directing.

Before long, my desire to perform was taking over my life. I was obsessed, getting up in the middle of the night when all the kids were asleep to make notes on the books or watch documentaries. I was now focussed fully on becoming an actress and doing whatever it took to get there. This was my chance to follow my dreams.

I researched acting classes in my local area and found one run by a TV casting director in Manchester. *She'll know what it really takes to make it in the business,* I thought, and signed up. They were evening courses, twice a week for two hours. Fortunately my friend Karen's niece came to babysit.

I couldn't wait to start the classes. It was so exciting to be back acting again and getting the chance to become different characters. We performed monologues in front of the class then got into pairs and acted out scenes together. Everything was filmed so we could watch it back together and hear everyone's notes.

The teacher was fantastic and very professional. She gave us feedback on our performance and warned us what to expect in an audition, how to act in front of the directors in castings for commercials and TV, and how to prepare a "self-tape", which is when you film yourself performing a monologue and send it to a casting director. Once the casting director from *Coronation Street* came in to give feedback on our performances. I was a bit nervous, but she complemented me on my "measured and engaging" performance. Her only criticism was to make sure that I sat a bit closer to the camera next time!

After the end of my course, I decided that it was time to put all this theory into practise and find some work. I did some more research online and found agencies that specialised in extra work. This seemed like a good place to start as you didn't need any professional experience to get walk on parts – or "supporting artiste" as they are more diplomatically called. I got taken on by an agency in Cardiff, who took some professional pictures of me and put me on the database. To my amazement, I got a job straight away. *This is it,* I thought, *my first professional role as an actress!*

Okay, I was only a "supporting artiste" but you have to start somewhere. There are so many stories of famous people who started their careers in this way. Sylvester Stallone was an extra in Woody Allen's 1971 film *Bananas*, playing a mugger in the subway. Renée Zellweger played a stoned freshman girl in 1993's *Dazed and Confused*. In the 1987 film *Less Than Zero*, Brad Pitt played a "Partygoer/Preppie Guy at Fight", for which he was paid the grand sum of thirty-eight dollars. Well, you've got to make a buck somehow! Ben Affleck and Matt Damon were walk-ons in *Field of Dreams* (1989), Megan Fox played a non-speaking dancer in a club scene in 2003's *Bad Boys 2* then Michael Bay cast her in his later films. In the 1950s, Clint Eastwood was an uncredited extra in lots of shows before he landed starring roles. The list goes on and on. Even Marilyn Monroe was an extra in her first-ever screen appearance, 1948's *Scudda Hoo! Scudda Hay!* She only had one line to speak of and not a very exciting one at that; "Hi Rad!"

But hey, if being an extra was good enough for Marilyn, it was good enough for me!

BABYMOTHER

After I left Shannon's Dad, I stayed at my mums for a year. So now I was nineteen, and back living in the village, which I had been desperate to escape. On the one hand, it was nice to be away from Justin and to be with my family, who were very kind to me and so good with the baby. But it was also painful to be there because all the memories came flooding back about losing my first love Rob and his friend Ed raping me, which I still hadn't told my family about.

So now it was just me and my daughter. *How am I going to live now?* I wondered. *What am I going to do?* I ended up getting a job in the bar at a nearby holiday camp. The long hours were daunting, but my parents looked after Shannon while I was at work. At the holiday camp, they had the legendary entertainers, the "Red Coats". I had heard about them because so many famous performers got their start working like this, Michael Barrymore, Johnny Ball, Des O'Connor, Jimmy Cricket, even Cliff Richard!

I was amazed at how much work was involved for the Red Coats. They had to be up for Kid's Club at 8am and entertain the children all day with arts and crafts or games. They'd get an hour off at 5pm to have dinner then be back in the club room by 6pm to do the bingo. At 7.30pm, they were up on-stage doing shows, dancing and singing all the way through until 1am. No wonder so many people with that kind of training went on to be so successful. It was a bit like being in a showbiz army!

As I watched the Red Coats day after day, I would think *I wish I could do that!!* I started to daydream about acting again. Well, if you don't dream it, you can't be it! I felt that seeing them was meant to be, but would it be possible for me to go into showbusiness now that had a baby? I realised how hard the Red Coats grafted, but I knew that I could work hard too. That was normal for me. In fact, I really enjoyed it; the only problem now was that I missed my daughter.

There were a couple of guys working behind the bar with me. One was called Nick, who was about three years older than me. He seemed like a nice enough guy, but I didn't really fancy him. He had a girlfriend at the time anyway. Plus, he liked to party a lot and we had completely different lifestyles. Although I was only young, I didn't enjoy life in a free-spirited way like most people my age; I didn't go out to drink and dance or get high. What happened with Ed and the rape had destroyed all that.

As time went on, Nick started to like me more and more. Although there wasn't that initial attraction, I was becoming fond of him too; he was good with his words and always worked hard, which I admired. He kept asking me out, but I said no as he had a girlfriend; if he wanted to be with me, he had to end it with her first. I wasn't expecting him to actually do it but, sure enough, he did, and we got together soon afterwards.

After nine months of dating, Nick and I decided to move in together. We rented a house in Hertfordshire, which was nearer to Shannon's father as we had shared custody of our daughter. Nick got a job in a bar, and I found employment in a newsagents. I worked hard as usual and, within a month, I was running the place!

However, almost straight away, I found out that I was pregnant. At first, I was shocked, but then quickly felt pleased about it. Nick didn't mind having a child either; he just went along with whatever I wanted. Fortunately, the birth with Maliki was without complications and he was a very easy baby who fed and slept well. He was always content. I used to take him to work with me at the newsagents, which the customers loved. Everything in life was plodding along okay apart from the fact that we didn't like the area where we lived. There were no job opportunities and there wasn't much going on socially – even the landscape was flat and boring!

Nick's friend lived in Cornwall and recommended that we move down there. When Maliki was six months old, we decided to give it a try. When we got to Cornwall, I trained as a nurse. Now, that was hard

– it made being a Red Coat look like a doddle! I went on to get a job in a care centre, which I enjoyed as I like looking after people. That's the mother in me, I guess. We stayed in Cornwall for a year and a half then I got pregnant again. However, life down there wasn't much more exciting than in Hertfordshire. There wasn't much for young families to do. Yes, you had the beach but because the weather wasn't great, even that was pretty dull. Plus, there were no opportunities down there so, if I was ever to get a career in entertainment, I needed to move on.

I found myself stuck; I didn't know where to go or what to do. Then fate intervened. Nick was a huge football nut; when he was younger, he was told that he could go professional, and he still played football five times a week. He supported Liverpool and, although I wasn't a big fan, I used to go to the matches with him. One day, Liverpool were playing Wrexham, so we went up there to see his team play. As soon as we arrived, I fell in love with the area. The landscape was stunning. There was an amazing openness and sense of space through the hills and surrounding countryside, but then, just twenty minutes away, you had the town of Cheshire, and forty minutes away, the city of Liverpool. There was much more to do with the kids here and a lot more opportunity in terms of work. Here, maybe my showbiz dreams could come true.

So, the day after the match, as we drove back to Cornwall, I said to Nick, "Let's move to Wrexham." He was up for the idea. Fortunately his team had won so he was in a good mood. Plus, he always went along with what I did. There was a sort of love in our relationship, but, to be honest, I mothered him. It felt more like he was my son, rather than my man. In three weeks, I had found somewhere to live in Wrexham and a full-time job in a local care home. I'm very spontaneous and decisive like that; if I want to do something, I'll go and do it instantly. I can't stand procrastination. Sometimes, this can be a problem, because I don't think things through properly. But I knew I'd made the right decision this time.

I started work the day after we moved up there, even though I was already three months pregnant. We got settled into our new life but, unfortunately, the birth with Felicity was very difficult. She went breech at the wrong point, so I had to have an emergency Caesarean section. I was so happy to have another baby though. I just love babies and I had a feeling that I was meant to have kids, like it was my destiny. I loved being pregnant because it was an escapism from my depressed life. To be honest, I also loved the attention I got for being pregnant and having a new baby. It was nice to have something special to look forward to.

Nick didn't mind having more children. He never said anything about it, he just went with the flow. But the next year and half were very hard. I was working as a nurse in the hospital. I'd get up at five in the morning, have breakfast and be out of the house by six. I'd have to drop the kids at the hospital creche then be on the ward by 7am until 9pm at night, three days a week.

Nick and I weren't getting on very well either. He didn't really do much with the children. He just worked by day then played football or video games at night. The baby stuff just stressed him out; he preferred kids when they were older and felt that you couldn't really do much with them when they were small. We never really spoke anyway; there was no real relationship or adult conversation between us. He wouldn't cheat on me, I trusted him with that, but there was no real love there.

But still, we kept on keeping on. Then, about a year later, I got pregnant again. I didn't mind, I had always wanted a big family. Looking back, I think I had children to mask the pain of what had happened to me in my youth. Every time I got pregnant, I felt special. Whenever I gave birth, I felt worthwhile. When I held that baby in my arms, I was overwhelmed by this amazing sense of love. It was total escapism, caring from this beautiful little baby that couldn't survive without you. You are completely needed.

When I had my children, I finally felt wanted. I didn't feel loved by Nick and, deep down, I didn't feel that real love for him either. But I adored motherhood, so I gave it my all and committed to being the best mum ever. But the birth with Harvey was also very difficult. Things were not moving quickly enough, so I was given drugs to induce the birth but still he didn't arrive. After two days of this, my body gave in. I was losing a lot of blood.

"He has to come out now otherwise I'm going to die!" I screamed at the top of my voice.

Then I collapsed, shaking uncontrollably. I was so exhausted, I couldn't take any more. I had to be rushed to the operating theatre there and then.

Harvey was born by Caesarean five weeks early. Afterwards, I was on the ward with all the other mums. I was so weak that I couldn't even pick Harvey up. They put me in a side room as they decided what to do with me. They knew I was low on blood. Harvey started screaming but no one could hear us. I tried to get up to tell someone, but I collapsed on the floor and the canula ripped out my arm. I was shouting for someone to come and help. In the end, they had to give me a blood transfusion.

I took Harvey home to care for him. But then, six weeks after giving birth, I got pregnant again. I think I was addicted to giving birth! The stupid thing was, Nick and I weren't even really together by this point. He had moved out just before Harvey was born. He went to live with a friend, he didn't even tell me where. He did try to get back with me, but I knew it wouldn't work. I just didn't love him; I blame immaturity on my part for the reason we were together in the first place.

I don't know why I even entertained having sex with him, as he was more like a brother to me or another child. But then, one night, he was over at my place. I was exhausted with all the kids and work and got upset with everything. He comforted me, one thing led to another, and I ended up sleeping with him. We used protection but I still got pregnant. I couldn't believe this had happened again. Guess my last little boy really wanted to come through.

LIGHTS, CAMERA, ACTION!

All that family drama with Nick seemed like ancient history now and the big moment had finally come – my first day on a film set. The film was a historical drama set in Victorian times called *The Black Prince*, in which I had an extra role as a well-to-do lady.

My friend Karen came around the night before to wish me luck.

"We need to sort out your hair," she said.

My hair was dyed blonde at the time, but my roots were black. They didn't have peroxide in the old days, so for period drama you had to have all one colour. I'd been so busy getting the kids sorted for the day that I hadn't even thought about it!

"Will you bleach my roots?" I asked.

"I don't need to do your roots," Karen replied. "I'll just put on a toner."

Karen popped to the shops, got the colour, and did it for me. But it came out a garish orangey yellow; it was hideous. Now the shops were shut so I couldn't get any more, and I was getting up at 4am before they opened again. Typical!

"Oh well, it will have to do," I said with a shrug.

That night, I was so excited, I could hardly sleep. I had to be up and out by 4.30am, but I had too much adrenaline to be tired. I got Karen's niece Jodie to babysit my children, so I knew they were in safe hands.

About 6am, I arrived on location; a grand, manor house in Cheshire. It was so exciting to see the big catering vans and all the lights and cameras being set up. What a buzz! The crew were all having breakfast and everyone was so friendly. After grabbing a coffee, I went in to see hair and make-up. I told the lady about what had happened with the dye; fortunately, she just laughed about it.

"Well, that's Sod's law, isn't it?" she chuckled. "We haven't got time to dye it now. Don't worry, we'll just stick a wig on you!"

She gave me a black wig to wear – not that different from my natural hair colour. Annoyingly, they had to take out my new hair extensions to fit it on, which I had just paid a lot of money to have done. Sod's law indeed!

When my hair and make-up was finished, I put on my costume – a long, brown, Victorian style dress. I was all dressed up and ready to go by 7am. But I had to wait until after lunch to do my scene. You get used to a lot of waiting on film sets. My role was as a posh lady, standing at the bar, drinking and chatting. As I was waiting for the filming to begin, I felt so happy; it was like my birthday and Christmas come at once. Finally, I was exactly where I wanted to be. It was so emotional, I felt like crying; I wanted this so badly. But I swallowed down the tears and focused on the scene. I didn't want to mess this up. I thought back to my acting training of how to block out the outside world, ignore the camera and all the people standing around, and enter into the mind of the character.

Finally, the crew were ready. The assistant director called for quiet and an eerie hush descended on the set. The director of photography said, "Camera rolling" and the director shouted, "Action."

It was quite surreal to finally find myself in this position. This was the moment I had been waiting for all my life. We had to do quite a few takes of the scene because the main actors kept messing up their lines. But I didn't mind; I was just taking everything in. It was a real eye opener as to what actually happened on set, how many takes they do and how they shoot from so many different angles. It was like being at film school!

Because I got such good feedback from that first shoot, the work from the agency came in thick and fast. My next job was to go to Barry Island for two days to be in the TV hospital drama *Casualty*. I didn't have any lines, but I had to walk behind the main cast, so it looked like a busy street. The definition of being a walk on!

I was so excited, but they turned out to be two of the hardest days of my life. The weather was horrendous; it hailed, sleeted and the temperature was minus three. But, because *Casualty* was filmed six

70

months in advance, it was meant to be June, so we had to wear summer clothes. What a nightmare; you're trying to look good on camera, but you've got all the wind and rain in your face so your skin turns blue and you look like a drowned rat. I was laughing to myself, thinking, *Is this really what you want to do? Why are you putting yourself through all this?*

But I still loved filming – even the weather couldn't put me off that! Most of the extras waited around in a portacabin all day, but I used the time to hang out with the main cast and crew. I watched all the different roles on set and listened in to see if I could gain any acting tips. I did some networking to build up my contacts too, which even lead to more work further down the line. Afterwards, the agency called me to say that the director really liked me so hopefully they would use me again. It's all about who you know in this game!

My next job was in Manchester, for a music video for the band *The Insiders*. I was supposed to be playing a prostitute. But when I got there, the director looked me up and down and shook his head in despair.

"You're too pretty to play a prostitute," he groaned. "We need someone rougher looking."

I didn't know whether to be offended or flattered! They didn't have time to find anyone else, so they covered me in hideous make up with these big black eyes and dressed me in a chunky, woolly coat with a sexy, red bra and tights underneath. In the video, I had to act as if I was having sexual intercourse with a werewolf. They hadn't told me about that bit! I came to realise that this was a common problem; the agency often sent you a brief for the role, but it wasn't really clear what you would have to do.

The guy I had to get off with was wearing one of the BBC's werewolf masks from *Doctor Who*. Doing a sex scene was really funny and nothing like what you'd imagine it to be. You're trying to be all sexy, whilst everyone around is giggling because it's so ridiculous. It was a real eye opener; I'd never done anything like that before. I didn't feel embarrassed though because, when I got into character, it wasn't me. In fact, it was fun to become this crazy, wild persona, not like me at all. It was a good challenge and they were such a talented production company that I learnt so much from them.

Not long after, I got another job on a music video. I had to go to Manchester again for the shoot, which was in a dark basement nightclub.

"Can you dance?" the director asked when I arrived.

"Yes, I do pole dancing," I explained. "And burlesque."

So, they dressed me in a white vest top and tiny, black shorts and put me on this podium. Then they started the music playback.

"Okay, you can start dancing now," the director shouted. "Action!"

And that was it – no choreography or direction or anything. Now, I'm not a professional dancer so this was way out of my comfort zone. But they were already filming so I had to just go for it.

The song had a heavy, fast beat, so I started wiggling and waving my arms about, in front of about fifty people. Everyone was looking at me, aghast, no doubt thinking, *What the hell is she doing?* They didn't say anything, but I knew for a fact it was bloody awful.

All through the day, they did loads of takes, putting different girls on the podium. The others were all proper, professional club dancers then there was me flinging my arms and legs about like a muppet. I couldn't wait for the director to call cut!

I wish I could say that was the only time I made a fool of myself on a job but far from it. Another time I was filming a TV drama in Leeds, on location in a public garden.

The main cast were walking through the park and I had to cycle past on a bike and accidentally barge into one of them.

Some of the other extras were walking dogs. After filming the scene, we had a break and one lady told me to hold her dog while she went to the toilet. While I was waiting for her to return, another extra came up to me.

"That's the director," he revealed, pointing to a man standing by the camera. "Why don't you go and make yourself known?"

So I went over to introduce myself, but the dog started pulling on his lead. He dragged me over so fast that I fell face first into the director's crotch. The female producer sitting next to him looked shocked. I got up and apologised and we all had a laugh about it in the end, thank God. But I noticed that they didn't hire me again.

Lord knows why but I seem to have a habit of embarrassing myself. Once, I got a job doing some presenting for a conference at the NEC in Birmingham. I was being filmed by a company talking about their new product; a QR code, which you scanned on your mobile phone, and it took you through to a website. They had printed the QR code on a T shirt for me to wear. But because I'm big chested, when I put it on, the QR code they had to scan was right on my nipple. How excruciating!

At least hardly anyone saw that footage. The most cringey experience was when I made a complete fool of myself in front of millions of viewers on ITV. I got chosen to be in the studio audience for a game show called *Pick Me*. I knew nothing about the show, but my friend and I heard they were looking for people and we thought it would be fun to go along.

When we arrived at the studio in London, the producers told us to sit in the middle seats at the front. They explained the format to us; three people were picked from the audience, the presenter asks them a question then has to guess if they're lying or not. If he thought you were telling the truth, you won £1000.

So, we sat down and they started the countdown to the show. *Three, two, one... action!* The presenter did his introduction then it was time for him to pick the contestants from the audience. We had been told to wave to get his attention, and to my amazement, he picked me, along with a young guy and another woman. As I made my way down onto the studio floor, I could feel everyone watching me. I was so nervous. I took a deep breath and tried to stay calm. *Don't trip over, for God's sake!*

We each stood at a podium. The first guy was asked his question and gave his answer. Then the woman heard her question and answered. When it was my turn, a new question came up. Now, because I had never seen the show, I hadn't properly understood the format. I thought that everyone was going to answer the same question. So, when I heard something different, I started to panic. *What on earth am I going to say?*

The question was "George Carver was an agricultural chemist who discovered three hundred used for ... WHAT?"

The night before, I had watched a documentary called *The Syphilis Experiment* where scientists had given a thousand people in the Third World syphilis, then tried to cure it. So when the chemist question came up, I blurted out, "Syphilis!" I do that sometimes; I know what I want to say but it comes out all wrong. Plus, I've always been rubbish at lying so I was the world's worst contestant for a show like this!

So that's how I ended up saying syphilis on national TV! The director had to call cut and stop filming; everyone was laughing so much, they were crying. They had to have a pause and reset before they started recording again. Still, on the upside, because I was obviously so rubbish at lying, when I did have the answer, the presenter knew that I was telling the truth, and I won the thousand pounds after all!

ROCK BOTTOM

It was a shock to be pregnant again so soon after having Harvey. But, with my Catholic background, there was no way I would get rid of the baby. As usual, Nick didn't really say anything and just went along with it. So, off we went again.

However, things were different this time. I was really poorly throughout my final pregnancy. The kids were excited about having another baby brother, but I was already so exhausted. I was breastfeeding Harvey whilst pregnant with Blake.

Some people that I met judged me for having so many children.

"I bet you're claiming benefits for all those kids," they said. "That's why you're having them."

But I earnt every penny I got. I was working all the time. My parents have always been hard grafters and so was I.

It was a difficult pregnancy and Nick did not make it any easier. By this stage, it was a constant battle between us. If I said I was tired, he would claim that he was even more exhausted and needed to crash out. If I asked for an hour to sleep, he would turn up after exactly an hour on the clock and say okay, I need to rest now. It was all so stressful. Then, after months of struggle, I had Blake nine weeks prematurely. He just couldn't wait to come out. Nick wasn't at the birth. When I phoned up to tell him that I was going into labour, he didn't believe me. It was like talking to a child.

When Blake was born he only weighed three pounds. He was so tiny, you could fit him in the palm of your hand. They placed him in a special baby care unit to keep an eye on him. It was so frightening, I was terrified that he was going to die. I was constantly crying but then I had all the other children to think about as well. I was going through all this on my own, with no family around. Nick was no help with the kids, he always claimed that he was too busy to take them.

"They're your kids," he sneered. "You deal with them. Why should I do it?"

He even accused me of going out on the town when I was staying in the special baby care unit with Blake!

So there I was, trying to battle it all out all alone. Of course, I was very happy that Blake was here, I have so much love for all my kids. But, when I was staying in the baby care unit, I realised that, despite all my children, I was still lonely. I'd never had post-natal depression before, but I started to get it after this last birth.

After eight weeks, I was finally allowed to take Blake home. I was so worried that he wasn't going to survive that I didn't let him out of my sight. One night, he was in the buggy by the fire in the living room. His breathing was very shallow, and he was white as a ghost. I knew there was something wrong with him, especially with my nurse's training. The health visitor came around and said to keep an eye on him. But then he went completely limp and stopped breathing completely. I called an ambulance and started to do mouth to mouth resuscitation on him.

The ambulance arrived and whisked us to hospital. At first, the doctor took a quick glance at Blake and declared that he was fine. But I knew there was a real problem and wouldn't let him brush me off like that.

"Look at him properly," I insisted. "I know that something is seriously wrong."

The doctor rolled his eyes as if I was a mad woman but, when he inspected him, Blake stopped breathing again and went limp. That made them panic and the doctors and nurses kicked into action. Thank goodness I had put my foot down. If I had been a first time mum or I hadn't had that knowledge from my nursing days, Blake could have died.

Fortunately, the hospital staff came through, and they rescued Blake. But the problems persisted, and we were back in hospital for another month. When we finally came home, everything hit me; the loneliness, the hard work and the anxiety about my child. I was so exhausted and had no one around to help me. A lot of people had let me down and I was feeling isolated. I had a couple of close friends, but they had their own lives to get on with so couldn't give me the support I needed.

It was all getting on top of me and I was sinking more and more into a pit of depression. I went to the doctors and they prescribed me anti-depressants, one a day. I took them religiously, but I still didn't feel any better. If anything, I felt worse. Over the next seven weeks, I became so down that I couldn't sleep or eat. I felt like a compete zombie.

One day, I called Tracey, my older friend and surrogate mum from back when I was living on the farm with Shannon's dad. I asked her to come up and stay for a while to help me. She was always such a loyal and supportive friend. When she arrived the next day, we had tea and a catch up, although I didn't tell her what was really going on inside.

"I'm just popping out," I told her. "Would you mind keeping an eye on the kids?"

She said that was fine, so I got in my car and just drove. I had no idea where I was going or what I was doing. I ended up in Warrington with no clue how I got there, sitting in a Morrisons' car park, just staring out of the windows for hours.

Then I drove to a Travelodge, booked a room for the night and stared at the wall. I felt numb. My phone kept ringing, but I kept cutting it off. No one could find me or get hold of me.

Finally, I sent a text to Tracey.

"I don't want to die but I can't cope anymore," I explained. "Sorry."

I took a handful of painkillers and lay down on the bed, waiting for them to kick in. I really didn't want to take my own life, but I didn't know what else to do. It was the worse decision I had ever made but I felt like there was no hope. In fact, I felt nothing. The depression was so overpowering, I couldn't think or feel anything. It was so horrible.

When Tracey received my message, she called an ambulance and got my phone tracked. They took me to hospital and pumped my stomach, then kept me in there overnight. I was in excruciating pain, but at least I was alive.

The next day, a psychiatrist was sent in to see me. She asked me lots of questions. At first, I panicked, thinking they were going to take my children away from me.

"Don't worry," she reassured me. "No one is going to take anyone from you."

I decided that, in order to get well, I had to trust her. So, I answered all her questions very honestly. I explained that my children were fine because I didn't leave them in any danger, but I had reached the end of my tether.

After a frank discussion, the psychiatrist gave me her diagnosis.

"There's nothing mentally wrong with you," she confirmed. "You're fine, you're not even really depressed. But you are completely and utterly exhausted."

A tear rolled down my cheek as she spoke. It was so comforting to be heard by this kind and compassionate woman. I felt like someone finally understood the situation I was in.

"It's a lot to cope with," she continued. "You're working full time and looking after the kids with no support. Anyone in your position would crack."

After I had spoken to the psychiatrist, I felt amazing, euphoric even. Now that I had spoken to someone about my problems, I had a new sense of freedom. It was as if the light within me had been turned back on again. *At last*, I thought, *I'm back to my normal self.*

I stopped taking the Citalopram, which also made me feel better. I wondered if these pills were actually the cause of me trying to commit suicide; that's what the psychiatrist implied at the hospital. I'm not a suicidal person – I would never do that and leave my children. But those tablets messed with my head and wouldn't let me sleep. Now I had stopped taking them, I could see just how horrible they made me feel. It's worrying to think what the wrong medication can make you do. Never again!

Reassured that I was fine to leave, the nurses discharged me from the hospital and put me in a taxi back to the Travelodge. I collected my car from the car park and drove back home. When I got back to the kids, I gave them a big hug – the biggest ever. Obviously, they didn't know what had happened, but it was a huge relief to be back with them again. Tracey threw her arms around me and said she was here to look after me. And, like a true friend, she did. She stayed for a few days and cooked for me and the children. She let me rest and I slept well for the first time in months, over twelve hours a night.

Of course, in the end, she had to go home. But I felt good now and I was looking forward to the future. This brush with death had left me feeling very lucky. From now on, I tried to focus on life in a new way. It was just like when I had that car crash which stopped my life and restarted it for the better. I was still alive. I was meant to be here for a reason. Now I just had to work out exactly what that was.

THE FIGHT BACK

Once I had recovered from my overdose, I couldn't believe I'd been so stupid. If I was gone, what would my kids do without me? They'd have no one; their dads were no help. I shuddered to think about what would have happened. It was a deep reality check. I knew that I had to forgive myself for what I'd done and put things into perspective. *We all get down sometimes*, I told myself. *Things happen, life can be tough.*

But it was over now, and I had to move on. Instead of focusing on the past, I turned my attention to what I did have in my life and what I'd achieved so far. I had five beautiful kids, a lovely home, some true friends and lots of dreams and ambitions for the future. Every day, I listed all the things for which I was genuinely grateful and gave thanks to the universe. I had been given a second chance. Now I had to use it.

I decided that things had to change for me. All my life had been quite dowdy up until that point. I had always just worked and had children; I hadn't really met anyone exciting or done anything much. I started to crave some adventure, but I didn't really even know what that meant or how to go about it. I never used to go out and instead just concentrated on the children. But the problem was that I lost myself, I wasn't my own person anymore. Even as a mum, you need your own space. That's so important, as any parent can confirm.

I realised that I needed to start taking some time for myself. It sounds like a strange place to begin but I decided that I was going to have hair extensions. I had always wanted to give them a go, but I could never justify spending the time or the money on them. Now, I decided it was the perfect moment; I deserved a treat and longed for a change. Maybe this was the place to start.

I went to the hairdresser's, who was a lovely girl called Davina. It took hours but she patiently wove in the blonde extensions, chatting to me about my life as she did. When she had finished, she picked up the mirror and showed me the results. Oh my God, I loved it! It completely transformed the way I looked. It really changed how I felt about myself too. For the first time ever, I looked in the mirror and liked what I saw.

"You look amazing!" she gushed. "You need to go out now and show off the new you!"

So, Davina invited me on a night out, which was something I never did. I paused for a moment; I had become so used to denying myself any fun or "me time" that, at first, I didn't think I could say yes. But then, I thought again.

"Okay, that sounds great. Let's do it!" I whispered and gave my lovely, long mane a shake – this was the new lioness me!

Later, I told Nick I was going on a girl's night out and asked him if he would look after the kids. Amazingly, he agreed, although I knew he would be phoning me up the minute that I said I would be back. So that Friday night, Davina and I got all dressed up and went to a local pub. We had a few drinks then went on to Wrexham for a dance.

As we entered Liquid Nightclub, there was a competition going on. There was a big stage set up with a guy from *Loaded* magazine, who was travelling all around the country to find Miss Loaded. When Davina and I went to the bar to get some drinks, the owner of the night club approached me.

"I think you should enter this," he urged.

"Oh God, no!" I gasped. Me in a beauty pageant? No way!

"Why not?" Davina replied. "You should definitely do it."

To be honest, I couldn't think of anything worse. I still wasn't very confident with my looks or my body – especially not after having five kids. I hadn't forgotten all that bullying back at school for being so ugly either.

But the nightclub owner was adamant.

"Go on, go for it!" he said, nudging me forward.

He even gave me two free shots for a bit of Dutch courage!

I never drank so, after that, my head was all fuzzy.

"Go on, Laura!" Davinia encouraged. "You can do it!"

"I'm not sure," I stammered. "Maybe ..."

I was still hesitating, when the club owner grabbed my hand and lead me backstage. Lots of girls were already waiting there – they were absolutely gorgeous. *What on earth am I doing here?* I thought. I felt so out of my depth. I had only just found out about the competition; they were all really done up in stunning dresses, full make up, and looked like they had been getting ready all day. I had just come for a girl's night out in an old purple number!

Next, the guy from *Loaded* came into the backstage room and described how the event would run.

"I'm going to take you out front one at a time," he explained. "The girl who gets the loudest cheer will win."

Oh my God, I thought. The bottom fell out of my stomach. I didn't realise they were going to take you out in front of everyone. There must have been about five hundred people out there!

The other girls nodded serenely as if they were expecting this all along, but I started to panic. My heart pounded in my chest, and I burst out into sweat. I didn't even have Davina with me at this point because she was waiting outside. *How do I get out of this now? Shall I just make a run for it?*

All these thoughts were rushing through my head so I could barely think. At that moment, a huge cheer went up from inside the club – the competition had begun. One by one, the *Loaded* guy grabbed the girls and walked them out onto the stage. The crowd were going wild. I looked over to the exit – maybe if I made a break for it now, I could get away. But, before I could move, the *Loaded* guy grabbed my hand. I'm surprised he could keep hold of it, my palm was so sweaty.

"You look great," he said. "Ready?"

Before I could reply with a resounding "NO!" he led me out onto the stage. As we walked out, hundreds of people turned to look at me. Not only that, but there were loads of photographers, who started taking shots. Snap, snap, snap! The flashes were dazzling. *This is it, I* thought, *it's too late to run now*. I just about managed to smile, but in my head, I was screaming, *Shit, shit, shit!*

As if she sensed my fear, Davina pushed to the front of the crowd and started cheering and clapping. Like a match in a tinder box, she seemed to set the others alight. Everyone was whooping and applauding. It was deafening. Afterwards, the *Loaded* guy lead me backstage then took out the rest of the contestants. When we had all had our turn, he called everyone out on stage at the same time. He told the crowd to cheer for the girl they thought should be *Miss Loaded* and walked past us one by one to gauge the audience reaction. To my astonishment, when it came to me, I got the loudest cheers.

Wow, I thought. *This is mind blowing!* It was such a euphoric feeling, one that I never thought I would experience. It was so bizarre; what they saw and how I felt were complete opposites. I didn't look at myself and think, *Oh yes, I'm beautiful, I could win this.* I had gone from being a particularly ugly girl that was bullied and teased non-stop to competing in a beauty pageant against really attractive women and even winning. I couldn't believe what was happening. I wiped away the tears welling up in my eyes – I didn't want my mascara to run now!

The guy put a tiara on my head and declared me *Miss Loaded* for the night. I had won the chance to go to London to enter the final competition. When I stepped off stage, Davina ran up and grabbed me. She was so excited and happy, but I was still in shock, just trying to take it all in.

At that moment, the nightclub owner came up to me with a congratulatory drink.

"Congratulations," he said and gave me a big kiss. "I knew you could do it. That's why I pushed you into it."

"Thank you," I replied and told him how grateful I was for his support.

He told me that he wanted to show me something and took me to the side of the bar, where there was a mirror.

"Look at yourself," he said, turning me towards the glass. "You're beautiful, you really are."

So that's what he wanted to show me – my own reflection! He could see my insecurities and anxieties and was trying to help me break free.

"Why don't you see it?" he asked. "What are you insecure about?"

Of course, he didn't know what I had been through, and I couldn't tell him now. I just thanked him for everything and went back to find Davina and celebrate.

But not for too long, of course, because I had to go home and pick up the kids; Nick was only prepared to have them for a couple of hours. He used to phone me to check where I was if I was just one minute late picking them up! When I got home, I tried to tell Nick what had happened, but he wasn't really interested. It didn't matter; this night was mine and he couldn't take that away from me.

About six weeks later, I was supposed to go to London for the final. But, typically, one of my children was poorly. Nick said he was too busy to look after them and, of course, the kids always came first. I wasn't that disappointed – I never wanted to be a beauty queen. These pageants weren't really me but the process of having faced my fear and succeeded helped me to turn a corner in my life.

From then on, my confidence grew. I was finally able to start to grow beyond that ugly little girl who was so badly bullied and hated the way she looked. I tried to think back to her and comfort her somehow. If I could have travelled back in time to tell her that one day she would win a beauty pageant, she would have laughed me out of the room. But as I looked at the photos the magazine sent of me in my tiara that night, I decided that it was truly time to let go of the vision of myself as an ugly duckling for once and for all. Now was the moment to become the swan, open my wings and take flight!

LUCKY BREAK

Over the next year, I got a lot more jobs as an extra, including working for many of the classic British soap operas. I was in the background of a club scene in *Hollyoaks*, a commuter in *Casualty* and a passer-by strolling through the park in *Doctor Who*. I even got cast as a nurse in *Emmerdale*; I had plenty of real-life experience for that role. It was weird to be back in the uniform again but only pretending to do the job. Much easier!

I appeared in the Sky Drama *Brassic* a few times, which was filmed locally, and I did a few commercials. I filmed in Croatia for a fitness app and had to bike down a super steep hill on my push bike, which was exhilarating. One of the funniest jobs I did was for a TV advert as a frenzied woman on heat chasing a man wearing Lynx deodorant!

I got some serious roles too, including in an ITV drama called *Anne*, about an inspirational woman who dedicated her life to campaigning for justice following her son's death in the Hillsborough football disaster. I played the wife of Michael, Anne's son, who was the brother of the boy that died and one of the main characters. I even had my own dressing room – I was really going up in the world! I also got to sit with the main cast. They were very friendly and gave me lots of advice, insisting that I had to get an agent who represented real actors now, not just "background artistes."

I knew they were right. Being an extra was a great start in the business but I wouldn't be satisfied with it forever. It was time to move to the next level. I remembered what the actor that I met in Spain had told me; I had to make a showreel. That way I could showcase my talent to agents, directors and producers, and demonstrate myself playing different roles.

I paid to get it done with a professional showreel company, which was very expensive. It isn't cheap to get started in this business! I wanted to show a range of performances, so I chose a sad scene about a woman whose husband is cheating on her and a gangster scene, in which I play a tough broad. The studios wrote the scenes for me. They sent me a copy to check that it was what I wanted, and I was pleased; it had the grittiness and range of emotion that I was looking for.

For the shoot, I went to the famous Pinewood studios in Buckinghamshire, just outside London. When I arrived at this majestic white building, I was so excited. Pinewood Studios is very famous in the business. For over eighty years, it has been the location for some classic productions of British cinema history from its first crime drama in 1936 called *Talk of the Devil* and early films like *The Red Shoes* (1948) to the saucy 1960s *Carry On* Films and the classic Bonds like *Dr No, Goldfinger* and *You Only Live Twice*. Not to mention the *Harry Potter* franchise and the recent *Star Wars* reboots.

These were the kind of films that I had grown up watching on TV with my mum and dad. To be filming my showreel here made me feel like I was part of cinema history. They even filmed *Lara Croft: Tomb Raider* there in 2001, the film which gave me my nickname at school! If only the school bullies could see me now!

On the first day, I met the two male actors I was to act alongside, so we could practise together and whip up some on-screen chemistry. The director had won awards for his short films and was very professional. We rehearsed in front of him, and he gave us notes on our performance, which was super helpful. That night, I stayed with my friend Tracey, who lives near London. She helped me run through my script and learn my lines. Well, she tried to, but she kept on cracking up. She was doing her best tough gangster voice, which was hilarious; it was hard to keep a straight face opposite that. She has known me for years and couldn't take me seriously as a badass at all!

The next day, I went back to Pinewood for 11am. Our studio was opposite the set for the latest James Bond film, which was very exciting. We had a coffee and talked through what was going to happen. The director looked through the costumes I had brought and helped me select the right ones. Then the hair and make-up lady got me ready, while the rest of the crew set up the room. In the first scene we filmed, I played a woman finding out that my husband was cheating on me. To get into the emotion, I drew on my past relationships; how much they had hurt at the time and what those men put me through. Personal experiences really help with acting – at least those exes came in use in the end!

Although I had been on set many times as an extra, this was the first time I was playing a main character. It's one thing watching other people act; when the focus is on you, it's completely different. I was so excited, my belly was doing somersaults. But it also felt right. *This is what I'm good at,* I thought, bigging myself up. It felt so natural for me to be in front of a camera and performing. *I should have been doing this years ago.*

After filming the first scene, we had a break and went for lunch in the café. They were filming *Star Wars* at the time, so I got to see lots of the cast and crew in there. I even had a chat with one of the stunt men. I told him that I was training for the stunt register, and he revealed that the job was very hard but well worth it.

After lunch, we performed the other scene, which was my favourite. I got to play a total bitch; the male character came in all hard but then I snapped the power away from him. It was so euphoric to embody that "don't fuck with me" energy. *I'm nice but if you cross me you've had it.* It was time for me to channel that in my real life! They made me up really heavily to play the gangster. But it was so hot in front of the lights that my make-up was melting. *Oh my God, I'm going to look like a clown,* I thought. I hoped that no one could see that I was sweating like a pig. *I'm going to pass out in a minute!*

The following week, the director edited the showreel and sent it over to me. It was strange to watch myself on screen. Although I was pleased with my performance, I didn't like the way I looked in the first scene; normally I wear eye make-up, but they didn't let me because it wasn't right for the character. In film and TV, you have to get used to that – what the director wants, goes. But I absolutely loved how I looked and came across in the second scene. I felt like a real Charlie's Angel!

Once the showreel was complete, I sent it out to acting agencies, including all the ones that the actor in Spain had told me about. I researched every company I contacted so I really knew all about them and personalised their letter. Of course, this meant that I had to write to everyone individually; I couldn't just copy and paste. In the end, I wrote to a good fifty or more agents. It took hours. And then I had to do something I hate; I sat back and waited.

Being passive isn't me at all but sometimes that's all you can do. I didn't hear back from any of them. Not one! They didn't even reply with a 'no'. I couldn't believe it; after all that hard work and expense of the showreel. *Will no one take a chance on me?* I licked my wounds and felt sorry for myself for a month or two. But then I picked myself up, went back to my computer and did the whole thing again. *There's no time to play the victim,* I thought. Of course, most of the agents still didn't reply. But then something wonderful happened; I heard back from a couple. *Finally, a lucky break!*

After researching the companies again, I decided to go with one that was based locally. The agent phoned me up and we had a nice chat. She asked me about my life; when I told her about the kids, she said that she could represent them too. At first, I wasn't sure about bringing them into the business. I didn't want them to get too disappointed. It's hard to cope with the rejection in this industry anyway but that's especially true for children, who often take things very personally.

At the same time, I think my brood are particularly talented – what mother doesn't? They're all so confident, especially Harvey who loves showing off to the camera. As long as I explained everything properly and prepared them for any disappointment, why shouldn't they have a go if they wanted to?

So, that night, I sat them down for a chat.

"You know mummy's doing acting?" I started. "Well, what would you say if you could do a bit too?"

"Yes please," they yelled, jumping up and down with excitement. "When can we start?"

"Hang on!" I said. "We'll have to go to the agency for a photoshoot. Then we can put you on the books and take it from there."

So, the next day, we went to Warrington to meet the agent and have our pictures taken. The kids were so excited; they couldn't stop yacking. We had to buy them all white T shirts and black trousers to wear, then they chose some other clothes too. We signed to say that we weren't represented by anyone else, then started the photoshoot. All the kids loved it and felt comfortable in front of the camera.

All except Blake, who wouldn't smile or turn around and kept pulling faces at the photographer. In the end, I had to resort to that special mothering trick – bribery!

"How would you like a piece of chocolate cake afterwards?" I asked.

"Maybe," Blake muttered, trying to play it cool.

But I knew that chocolate cake was his kryptonite!

"Well, just smile for the camera then we can go and get some."

"Okay."

The rest of the shoot went without a hitch and we all ate big pieces of cake on the train home. It was a brilliant day and so fun to do as a family. What an adventure!

On our way back, I was just as excited as the kids. *This is it, I'm finally going to make it!* I thought it would be easier now that I had proper representation as an actor, and the agency were going to get me so much work. How naïve I was!

NO BUSINESS LIKE IT

A month or two went by and we didn't hear anything. Then finally, my agent called.

"Great news, Laura, I've got you a job. Do you want to accept? It's for tomorrow."

It's difficult to do things last minute when you're a single mum with five kids. But it was always short notice in this game.

Fortunately, my friend's niece Jodie was available to babysit so I was able to take it on. It was a small part in a futuristic TV series called *The Feed,* which is on Amazon now. I played a "hub worker" with a chip in my head, who had to bike into work in the hub. The morning of the shoot went well. We kept biking along, doing the same thing again and again. Luckily, though, the weather was warm, and we were filming outside in Anglesey, which is one of my favourite places in the world.

Then, at lunchtime, things got really exciting. Two guys bought in an amazingly futuristic car, a Mercedes worth two and half million pounds. Wow! I love vehicles and went over to chat with them. When I told them about my stunt training, they asked me if I wanted to have a go in the car. Yes, please! I leapt in the car and drove it around the car park; well, the car was so hi tech, it drove itself. The guys were very nervous though and kept telling me to be careful. Inside, it had armchairs and even a flat screen television in the car door. It was so space age, I loved it. Getting back into my old banger would be a come down after this!

The next job I received was appearing in a pilot for a dating show called *Stand By Your Man* for Channel Five. I was single at the time so agreed to do it – unfortunately! It was absolutely awful. Forty women chose who they would like to date out of four guys and lined up behind them. Then each man picked one of those girls to get into a bed with him and ask him personal questions, like what was his favourite sexual position. It was so embarrassing.

Out of the forty women, the guy picked me, so I had to interview him. I was getting flustered as I don't really talk about stuff like that because of my Catholic upbringing. I didn't fancy him at all, but he kept making lewd references to my tattoo; at the time, I had a Playboy tattoo on my shoulder. Yuck! When I was sixteen, I went to Great Yarmouth seafront and got it done. It's covered up with a butterfly now. Fortunately, as this was just a pilot, I didn't have to go on a date with the guy and the programme didn't get aired. That was a lucky escape because by all accounts it was one of the worst things on TV and a huge flop. One woman on Twitter said that it was disgusting how the man walked down the line of women and picked them out like fruit!

The months went by and, although the agency got me some more extra work, I didn't get any auditions for decent roles. Ironically, Blake, who hated the photo shoot, got the best jobs. His first was on *Years and Years*, an ITV drama series starring Emma Thompson. Blake played the main character Russell as his younger self and was in about five scenes. He didn't have lines but was in full focus on camera for the first part of the show.

However, when the hero was young, he shaved off his hair. So, I had to convince Blake, who was six at the time, to shave his head. Of course, he didn't want to because he thought he'd look like an idiot.

"Don't worry, it'll be fine," I assured him. "It will grow back."

Eventually, he agreed to. But it was quite traumatic for him until he got an X box gift card from me!

I was filming that day, so Jodie took him, then there were people on set dedicated to looking after the child actors. This was Blake's first acting experience, but he was a natural. Out of all my kids I thought he would hate it, but he thoroughly enjoyed himself. It was birthday party scene, so he got to eat chocolate cake too. Afterwards, the casting director sent me a message to say what a lovely, well-mannered boy Blake was, very good at taking direction and a credit to the programme. That was nice because it made me feel that, even though I had allowed the kids to do acting, I was still doing my job a mother properly.

Since then, out of all the kids, Blake has got the most work. Funny how that happens. He did background work in the TV series *Ridley Road* and appeared in *Brassic* and *Deep Water*. He loves being on camera now and wants to be an actor. Unfortunately, Shannon was a bit more difficult – well, she was a teenager! While I was in Anglesey for *The Feed*, the agency called to ask if Shannon could do two days filming in Manchester on *Brassic*. She would have to wear the same school uniform both days.

She was sixteen at the time and had been badgering me for years.

"Mum, I want to be an actress just like you," she insisted.

"Okay," I said. "I'll give you a chance."

As I was away, I hired Jodie to take Shannon to the shoot; she had to be on set at 6am. Filming always starts very early. Although it was going to cost more for me to pay Jodie than Shannon was going to earn, it didn't matter. It would be a good start in the industry.

So, Jodie drove Shannon to Manchester, while I was filming in Anglesey. When I wrapped for the day, I phoned Shannon. I had to stay in a hotel that night as we had an early start the next morning.

"How did you get on today?" I asked.

"It's boring, Mum!" she whined.

I don't think Shannon realised that filming can be tedious; it's a lot of sitting around, doing the same things over and over again. It's hard work too – you're on and off set all day, doing take after take. It's definitely not as glamorous as it looks.

"Sorry you found it like that," I offered. "Hopefully tomorrow will be better."

"I don't have to film tomorrow," Shannon declared. "The director has said that's a wrap today, you don't need to come back."

I was surprised to hear this news.

"Are you sure?" I said. "The agency told me that you have to be there for two days."

"Yes, Mum, I'm sure," Shannon confirmed. "See you when you get back."

She hung up, then Jodie phoned me.

"Shannon said she's not needed for tomorrow, is that right?"

"Well, that does happen sometimes," I explained. "They might finish in one day."

"That's fine then," Jodie said. "If I'm not needed to take Shannon to Manchester tomorrow, I'll take my car to the garage to be fixed."

I should have questioned it more, but I didn't finish shooting until nine that night and needed to go to bed as I had to be up again at five.

The next morning, I was on set early and ready to film. Then, at 6.30am, I got a phone call from the director of *Brassic*.

"Where's Shannon?" he snapped.

"She said that she finished yesterday."

"No, she isn't finished," he yelled. "Where the fuck is she? If she doesn't come in, all the scenes from yesterday will have to be re-shot!"

"I'm so sorry," I soothed. "She said it was a wrap and she wasn't needed today. Don't worry, I'll sort it out."

So, I phoned up Shannon, who was asleep. When she finally woke up and answered the call, I was furious.

"You lied to me, Shannon," I yelled. "If people think our family are going to let them down, it'll ruin it for all of us. None of us will get any work."

Of course, Shannon just protested her innocence and said that she thought she wasn't needed.

"Well, we have to get you there NOW!" I declared.

The problem was, Jodie couldn't take her because her car was in the garage. So, I phoned my good friend Jack. He wasn't happy about it but as a favour he went to pick up Shannon at 7am. But at the Chester roundabout, his car broke down. Sod's law again!

By now, the *Brassic* producer was calling me, screaming blue murder.

"Where's Shannon? We're supposed to be filming by now. This is ridiculous. She'll never work in TV again!"

Jack manged to fix his car and got Shannon there for 9am. I put fifty pounds in my daughter's bank account so that she could get train home after she had finished for the day. It's very easy route. Then I turned my phone off and started working myself.

Brassic finished filming at 1pm. At 2pm, I finished shooting. When I checked my phone, there were about thirty missed calls. Shannon had been telling the director and crew that she didn't know how she was going to get home or who was picking her up. My phone was going crazy; I was getting calls from everyone. The agency was ordering me to get Shannon to leave. I explained that she had the money to get a train, but she was claiming that she couldn't because she was too scared. It was bizarre because she got the train on her own all the time!

Then the runner called and started shouting at me.

"She needs to go. The director has taken me out of the shoot to look after her. I'm not here to babysit!"

Then the director himself rings again. I explained to him that I was still in Anglesey filming, so I couldn't pick her up myself, but Shannon is sixteen years old and can get the train by herself. He said that she was now crying and complaining that I was being nasty, and I don't want her anymore. Wtf!

Of course, Shannon wasn't answering my calls. At 3pm, she texts me to tell me that her friend's mum was coming to pick her up "in the hour". But this lady didn't arrive until 5.30pm so the crew were calling me in a fury all afternoon.

"For God's sake, get Shannon off the set!"

The runner had to babysit her for three hours in the end!

When I finally got home, Shannon still claimed that she wasn't to blame. Somehow, it was all my fault – it always is mums, after all! She stuck to her story that the director had told her she had wrapped. I knew it was just that she didn't want to go back because it was hard work and boring and she couldn't have her phone on set. You know what kids are like.

I phoned the agent to do some damage limitation. I asked her not to let this affect her view of us all because she knew how reliable we were. But I asked her to please take Shannon off the books, which she did. That casting director would never have Shannon back anyway;

who could blame him? Fortunately, he was okay with me and the others though.

In the end, Shannon apologised to me and the agency. Then a few months later, she had three days on *The Irregulars*. She turned up on time for all the days and really enjoyed it. But I don't know if she's got the work ethic to become an actress. It's not all waltzing around in pretty frocks. My other kids just did a little bit of acting. Harvey only had one job in *Deep Water*, a psychological thriller film. I was working again that day, so Jodie took him to the set, and he was very excited. He loved the attention and still wants to be an actor today.

Unfortunately, poor Felicity hasn't had any roles yet. She was really upset, which was the very reason I resisted bringing the kids into the business.

She kept asking, "Why doesn't anyone want me?"

I explained that she wasn't exactly what they were looking at this moment, she just had to be patient. Although Flic hasn't had any film work yet, she is brilliant on stage. In film and TV, the camera does most of the work for you, but in theatre you have to be really expressive and larger than life. It's the opposite of filming. Flic's school has its own theatre, where she performed in *Beauty and the Beast*. She even sang in front of a big crowd in Llangollen pavilion for the *Eisteddfod* Welsh Day celebrations.

However, I was still having problems getting cast. My agent explained that, because of my age, she was sending me up for characters aged 35 – 45, but because I looked so much younger, I wasn't getting picked. I've always looked young. Maybe it's because I drink lots of water and eat quite cleanly. I don't drink or smoke, my fitness is good, and I always take my make up off, moisturise and exfoliate every night.

When I went to Barry Island to film *Casualty*, I took the train. As I went to buy my ticket home, the kind old lady at the ticket office helped me.

"Do you have a rail card, darling?" she asked.

I told her I didn't.

"Didn't your parents help with that?" she continued. I didn't know what she was talking about.

She took a photo of me and made me up a railcard.

"Oh, you're so cute aren't you," she cooed. "Here you go, love, have a good journey home."

I was cold and tired after filming, so I just paid for the ticket and went to get on the train. When I looked at the railcard, it was for ages 16 – 25. I look pretty confused in the picture because I had no idea what was going on!

I get women trying to mother me like that a lot, which is sweet. Makes a change from doing all the mothering myself! It happened last year, when the Jehovah's Witnesses came around the house.

"Hello, dear, are your parents in?" they asked when I opened the door.

"They probably are," I replied, thinking that my parents were usually at home. "Why?"

"Can you go and get them, please dear?"

"Not really, they live in Suffolk."

I wasn't taking the piss, I just didn't get what they were saying.

"Well, are your parents or guardians here?" they continued.

Now I understood where they were coming from.

"I am the parent!" I explained. "I own the house."

"But you look far too young to be in charge of a property."

"I'm actually over thirty."

"Oh, sorry, dear. I didn't think you were that old at all!"

When I go out with the children, everyone thinks that I'm their sister or nanny. No one believes I've got five kids. Once, I went in to see my daughter at school and a teacher ushered me into a classroom.

"Your exams are about to start," he yelled. "Come on!"

You'd think that looking young was a good thing. But now I realised that, as an actress, it was actually holding me back!

As the agency weren't coming through with much work, I signed up to a casting website called Star Now. I got approached by an ex-footballer called Evan. He was putting together a reality TV show like The Only Way Is Essex or Made In Chelsea, all about football players and their lives behind the scenes. He had signed up lots of reality TV stars from Love Island and other programmes, who were going to create a football team and play matches to raise money for charity.

Evan had seen my showreel and asked me to do a self-tape. Most people want that these days. I sent one off and Evan asked if I would like to present the show. Wowee! I was ecstatic. I had dreamt of being a presenter from a very early age. Once when I was ten, my folks took me to Blackpool for the day. At the seafront, I got my dad to film me on his mobile talking into a pretend microphone just like I was a presenter on location!

So, I travelled down to London for the filming. In the back of my mind, I had some anxieties that perhaps Evan was like some of those photographers in my modelling days and he was going to try it on. But, to my relief, he wasn't like that at all; everything was extremely professional. I got to interview all the celebrities and the footballers, which was fantastic. I felt proud that I had done a really good job. Finally, I was getting the break I deserved.

LOVE BOMBING

Back in 2012 the success in the *Miss Loaded* competition gave me a much-needed confidence boost. I was feeling happy with myself again and seeing life from a whole new perspective. I was twenty-seven, Blake was six months old and I had lost the baby weight. All my friends told me how good I looked and encouraged me to get back into modelling, so I decided to give it a go. I joined a website called *Model Mayhem* and received several offers straight away. I did quite a few fitness and underwear photoshoots and some glamorous ones in swanky, evening gowns. I loved being back in front of the camera. I felt so comfortable in my own skin and quite euphoric. I certainly wasn't looking for another relationship.

However, a couple of months later, I met another guy. Looking back, I should have spent longer on my own. It was too soon for me to be with someone, and I was still very vulnerable. But only retrospective vision is 20/20. At the time, it seemed magical. I went to a children's birthday party and met a great guy called Tom, a friend of a friend. He had two kids and one on the way with someone else, who he was no longer with. You'd think that would have been enough to warn me to stay away. But like the moth to the flame, I couldn't help myself. I guess I was still looking for that validation from someone else.

When I met Tom, he seemed so perfect. He fell in love with me at first sight and claimed that I was the woman he'd been waiting for all his life. He put me on a pedestal and was always there for me. He treated me like a queen, sending me flowers and making big displays of affection. If I ever needed anything, he would get it for me straight away and do anything for me. It was almost too good to be true.

All these should have been big red flags. I did think it seemed very quick for him to fall in love but, having been so bullied and abused for so long, it was music to my ears. Now I realise that he was just telling me what I wanted to hear. But back then, I didn't know anything about narcissists and the techniques they use to draw you in like love bombing, idealization and psychological manipulation. I'm afraid to say that I know only too well now.

For a year, I felt like the luckiest girl in the world. Tom gave me everything I could want in a relationship; he was great fun, cooked and cleaned for me, took me on lovely dates, helped out with the kids. This was when I was working as an auxiliary nurse at the local hospital, whilst getting back into modelling. Tom couldn't encourage me enough and supported me in all my dreams. I thought, *I've finally got my life back on track.*

At some point in that first year, there was a death in his family. At the wake, I met Tom's parents. They were very polite to me but, when Tom went out of the room, his dad shocked me.

"I'm not being funny, Laura," he said. "But I don't want to get to know you because I know what my son is like."

What does that mean? I wondered. *Is he implying that Tom had loads of women or something?* Well, even if he had played the field a bit, I knew that Tom couldn't have loved them like me. He worshipped me so much I knew that he would never leave me.

Later that day, his sister told me, "Just be careful of Tom, he's got a temper."

I had no idea what she was talking about; Tom was so gentle with me. Although they had warned me off him, I just couldn't see it at all. As we were driving home, I told him about it, but he just brushed it off.

"Oh, they're all just out to get me," he sneered. "I'm nothing like that."

Like a fool, I believed him and thought no more about it.

Then one day, my children went off with their dads for the day. Tom said that we should take this opportunity to have a nice day out, just the two of us.

"Why don't we go to the Sea Life Centre?" he announced. "It'll be fun."

"Yes, let's do it!" I exclaimed.

I loved days out and doing something different. I was usually too busy being a mum, but this sounded like a chance to be a big kid myself.

"Great!" Tom laughed. "Jump in the car and let's go."

But the moment we started driving, Tom suddenly turned.

"I've been thinking about it, and I don't want you being a model," he announced.

"What?"

I couldn't believe what I was hearing. He had always been so supportive of the idea up until now.

"Well, I'm still going to do it," I declared.

"No, you're not."

He shouted and became very angry. I'd never seen him like that before. It was a shock. We ended up having a huge argument. I asked him to stop and let me out of the car, but he wouldn't. Instead, he sped up and started driving like a mad man. I was scared; I'd had one bad crash before, I didn't want to be in another one.

Tom wouldn't stop screaming so I put my headphones in my ears to block out the sound.

"Right, I'm pulling over," he yelled.

He swung the steering wheel so suddenly that I jolted forwards, which really hurt. When the car stopped, he ripped the headphones out of my ears.

"Don't ignore me," he cried. "You will listen to me. You're not the person I thought you were. I'm not putting up with this."

Then he got out and kicked the side of the car, hard. His face was so red, he looked like he was going to explode.

What's happened? I thought. I couldn't understand how someone could change so much. Who is this ranting, controlling bully? Where has my devoted lover gone?

I got out of the car and stood there quietly for a moment but he sweet-talked me and persuaded me to get back in. As he drove off again, he started apologising.

"I'm sorry, I lost my temper," Tom muttered. "I didn't mean to. It will never happen again."

I accepted his apology and we drove on in silence. We went to the Sea Life centre for the day, and it was okay. But it wasn't really. Over the next year, he went from bad to worse.

I was offered a job on a lingerie shoot by a photographer who was starting up a business. He wanted to do boudoir shoots for wives to give their husbands as a wedding present. They were sexy but tasteful and artistic. It would be perfect for my portfolio and the pay was good too.

When I told Tom, he went ballistic.

"I don't want you doing it, Laura. You're not showing off your body. I don't want anyone else looking at you!"

I was completely taken aback. I didn't understand where all this jealousy had come from; he knew how loyal I was. Now I realise that he was trying to undermine the very core of who I was. He was trying to take away the thing I had a passion for and make me feel worthless. He claimed that he didn't want me to do modelling because it was degrading to women. But then he would always comment on women's bodies in magazines or on TV.

There were more outbursts like this all the time. One evening, I did a promotional job in a nightclub, selling shots of coloured vodka in test tubes. As I left the club, I walked to my car. Suddenly, Tom jumped out from behind the bus stop. He had been spying on me all night to try and catch me doing something "wrong" like talking to another man.

"I've been waiting for you," he sneered.

He looked so angry, it really scared me. I ran to the car, but he followed me, shouting abuse.

"I saw you with that guy, kissing him. D'you think I'm dumb?"

I had done absolutely nothing. I don't even flirt with men. Maybe it's my Catholic upbringing, but I'm the least sexy behaving girl out there!

"What on earth are you talking about?" I gasped. "What's wrong with you?"

I tried to reason with him, but he wouldn't listen. I wanted to go home but he wouldn't let me drive off and kept banging my car. I beeped my horn to get some attention from passers-by, and eventually, he left.

I drove away and went home. But, not long afterwards, he turned up at my house. Unfortunately, I opened the door and he stormed inside.

"How dare you humiliate me and do that?" he yelled.

I took a deep breath and turned to him, calmly.

"I think we should separate. I don't want to stay with you anymore."

"Well, you bloody well are," he snorted. "No one else's going to want you. You've got five kids."

I groaned. Now where had I heard that one before?

"I'm the only one that's here for you. You'd be nowhere without me."

After another hour of all this, he turned it all around and started being nice again. We went upstairs and made it up – sort of. Things were fine for a few days then that weekend, we went on a big night out together. Big mistake!

We went to Liverpool to see the comedian Jimmy Carr live. He was absolutely hilarious, and we were sitting right down the front, in prime seats. Then he got to the bit of the show with audience participation. He needed a volunteer and asked if anyone had ever done any acting. I raised my hand and, as I was the only woman who did, he picked me.

Jimmy got me and another guy up on stage and we all had a bit of banter.

"What do you do?" Jimmy asked.

"I'm a nurse," I revealed. "But I do a bit of modelling too."

"Oh yeah, I've seen that magazine!" the other guy quipped, and everyone laughed.

Then Jimmy gave us a script to read on stage. We had to act out a scene, which was really corny and funny. Afterwards, everyone gave us a round of applause and I sat back down. I looked over at Tom; he seemed fine, and we watched the rest of the show, which was brilliant.

At the end of the performance, we went around to the stage door to get Jimmy Carr to sign our programme. As the comedian came out of the theatre, he looked at me and smiled then he turned to Tom.

"What the fuck is she doing with you, mate?" he quipped.

It was just a joke, so I laughed then congratulated Jimmy on the show and got his autograph.

And that was that. Or so I thought. But when we got into the car, I could see that Tom was fuming.

"You alright?" I asked.

"Look at this girl on my phone." he replied, showing me a picture of some model. "She looks fit, doesn't she?"

"Okay," I replied, "but I don't know why you're showing me that. If I did that with a picture of a bloke, you'd go mad."

At that moment, Tom totally lost it.

"What the fuck do you know? You're too good for me now, I suppose. Now Jimmy Carr likes you!"

I couldn't believe how childish this was.

"What? This is ridiculous! He's just a comedian having a laugh!"

But Tom was livid, the veins looked like they were going to burst out of his head. He started driving at one hundred miles an hour, speeding round corners and overtaking like a nutter, even on blind bends. *Oh my God*, I thought, *he's going to kill me,*

He drove like a lunatic, and we got back to mine in record time.

I decided to just go home on my own and never have him in my space ever again. Thank God I hadn't moved in with him.

"I've had enough of this now," I declared. "Enough is enough."

I let myself in the front door, but he pushed his way in after me.

"Go home, Tom," I shouted.

I begged him to go but he wouldn't leave, so I realised that I would have to, even though it was my house.

"I'm going to Karen's for the night."

"No, you're not!"

I didn't reply, but just went upstairs to pack an overnight bag. *This man's not right,* I thought, *there's something seriously wrong with him.* I remembered what his family had told me that day.

Then, while I was in the bedroom, I heard the front door locking. *Oh shit, here we go! What the hell is he going to do now?* And then everything went very dark.

THE NARCISSIST

For a moment, I had no idea what had happened. I tried the light switch, but it wouldn't go on. *Damn, has the bulb gone?* I thought. I went into the bathroom, but the light wouldn't work in there either. *Hang on a minute...*

I realised that Tom must have turned off the electrics. *What a nutter!* I presumed he was downstairs, so I went out to the hallway and shouted out to him.

"Where are you, Tom? What are you doing?"

But there was no answer.

"Tom, can you hear me? Where are you?"

Again, there was silence. Now I became scared. Did he do it or had something serious happened? I had to get out of here.

I dashed back to the bedroom and looked out of the window. It was pitch black outside and there was no one around. *I'm going to have to jump out of the window,* I decided. I opened the window and started to climb out. Then, suddenly, Tom burst into room, shouting. It was like something out of *The Shining. Here's Tommy!*

Tom ran over, grabbed hold of me and pulled me back.

"Where do you think you're going?" he screamed.

"Leave me alone, Tom!" I cried.

I went to the door, but Tom blocked it.

"You're not going anywhere," he yelled.

Then he punched me and pushed me to the ground. He pinned me down so hard that my wrists were bruised. I tried to push him off and stand up, but he kicked me, making my legs black and blue.

"You look half decent when you get tarted up," he ranted. "But who'd want you with no make-up? You're so fucking ugly!"

"What are you on about?" I replied, staying to stay calm. "Look, I just I can't be with you, Tom. You've got problems."

It was like a switch had flipped in Tom and he couldn't stop shouting. "God, you're a horrible person. You're such a fucking bitch."

He went on and on like this, saying the same things over and over. We were arguing all night.

In the end, I had to back down, just to get some peace.

"Okay, I'll stay," I stammered.

But he was very clever and twisted everything around. He took what happened to me in the past and turned it against me.

"You're messed up in the head, no wonder you tried to kill yourself."

He made me believe that I was in the wrong. Even though he had abused me and I was covered in bruises, he made me think it was my fault. He tried to convince me that I was going mad, and he very nearly succeeded.

The next day, whilst I was at work, Tom stole my mobile phone and used it to call my dad. Tom went outside and locked me in the house so I couldn't stop him. I went to the kitchen, opened the window and listened in.

"I'm worried about Laura and concerned for her safety," Tom whispered. "I don't know what she's going to do to herself or the kids."

He was trying to convince Dad that I was insane and needed to be sectioned.

Unfortunately, because he always came across as a doting boyfriend, my dad thought Tom was honest and believed him. He was obviously asking what they should do. Because they lived quite far away, my parents didn't see Tom very often. As he had always been so nice to me in front of them, they didn't know any better.

I went upstairs and used the landline to call my mum on her mobile.

"Mum, Tom's calling Dad from my phone. He's trying to get me sectioned!"

Tom was so convincing that even she had believed him.

Afterwards, Tom hid my phone and came back inside. I tried to reason with him, but he wouldn't listen. So, I went back upstairs and called the police from the landline. While I was talking to them, Tom came into the room and tried to grab the phone off me. Too late – I had already given my address.

Not long afterwards, two policemen turned up. Tom had no choice but to open the door to them. I was still upstairs, so the police came into the room to find me. I told them what Tom had done to me and showed them the bruises. They arrested Tom and took him to the police station. I found where he had hidden my phone and called my dad to tell him what was really going on.

The moment he was released, Tom started frantically texting me.

"I'm so sorry," he said. "We can sort this out. We need to talk."

"There's nothing to talk about," I replied.

But he kept on and on.

"I can't be without you, Laura. I love you."

Over the next couple of days, he kept apologising, but I wouldn't budge. In the end, I collected all his stuff from my house and went to see him at a mutual friend's place.

"I really do love you," he begged. "When I was in the cell, it made me think. I'm so sorry. I'll never do it again."

I felt like I was stuck in a time loop – knowing that I didn't want to be treated like that but also craving the way that Tom had made me feel in the beginning. I found myself accepting the status quo because my brain couldn't see any other way. Even when I got out it felt like I was withdrawing from a drug and the only way to feel better was to get back what we had at the beginning. Something he promised would happen. It is hard to explain now why I went back, maybe being stuck was just what I knew and the world outside that situation seemed too big and scary to contemplate.

After that, we got back together but things just got weirder and weirder. It was as if Tom was trying to take full control of my life. It was absolute hell, but somehow I couldn't let go and move on. He made sure of that by being on my case all the time.

"Where are you?" he'd ask constantly. "What are you doing? What are you wearing?"

Of course, I didn't like it, but I just went along with it for an easier life. Or so I thought but in reality, it was anything but easy.

Over the next six months, Tom tried to push my friends away from me.

"You're not going out with them," he announced. "I don't like them. They're no good for you."

He tried to turn me against everyone and isolate me. He told me that my friends didn't like me and that his mates couldn't stand me either. When I fought back and declared I would do what and see who I wanted, he flipped and acted all sweet again.

"I'm just worried that they're not really your friends," he gushed as if he was doing all this for my sake. "I'm the only one who really loves you. Nobody cares for you like I do."

About two months after he got arrested, the court case came up. I was meant to go in to testify so Tom was on my case for weeks beforehand, begging me not to go in.

"I'll lose my job," he moaned. "And my kids. Do you really want me to lose everything?"

Then he started being nice and, yet again, I got sucked back in. *Maybe he will be okay, and everything will be fine now,* I thought. *It'll be like the good old days.*

In the end, I didn't turn up to court. Tom just went in and said that I lied about what had happened, which was why I wasn't there. After that, life was good for a couple of weeks, then his mood swung again. I felt like such a mug for not going to court. But by this point, my head was so screwed up, I didn't know what I was doing.

Of course, Tom fuelled this confusion. He even made me go to the doctors to check if I had a personality disorder. The doctor listened to me talk about my work and the kids then gave me his professional opinion.

"You have a lot going on," he said. "No wonder you're exhausted. Do you have a partner?"

I told him about Tom and his erratic behaviour.

"Ah, now I see," the doctor said, nodding. "It's not you. *He* is your problem."

Tom contacted my friends and claimed that he was concerned because there was something wrong with me. But my four true besties knew this wasn't right; I would never shut them out like that. They knew I'd speak to them if I was having a breakdown like before.

So, they got together and came around one night to find out what was happening. When I told them the truth, they were shocked. Even Karen said that Tom seemed so nice, she would have never expected all this from him.

"This is getting out of order now," she declared. "Something needs to be done."

It was like an intervention. I agreed with them; I didn't defend Tom. But even though I knew that that I needed to leave him, I still didn't. I felt that I couldn't live without him. Despite all the suffering, I just couldn't break away.

THE CYCLE OF ABUSE

Anyone who has been in an abusive relationship with a narcissist will recognise the pattern that I went through. The transformation from the lovely, kind person that you met to an angry, controlling monster is disturbing. You keep waiting for your partner to return to that funny, attentive lover. And for a moment they do, only to lull you into a false sense of security before they switch back again. It's like *Jekyll and Hyde*.

It's so confusing. You don't understand why they have changed, so you start questioning yourself. This is the most dangerous part; now you don't even trust your own judgement. *Is it me?* You think as they continue to be nice in front of everyone else. *Is all this my fault? Am I doing something to anger them?* Of course, this is the very effect the narc is going for. They're so clever at manipulating your mind.

When I was with Tom, I'd never heard of "gaslighting", that horrible technique when someone makes you question your sanity, perception of reality, or memories. Now I know it's a deadly and all too common form of psychological abuse. I didn't know I was experiencing the classic narcissist/empath relationship. I didn't realise that my situation with Tom was so typical and that there were millions of victims like me out there.

Narcissists thrive on drama and getting attention, whilst empaths have compassion and understanding; too much. In a way, they are opposites and opposites attract but not always in a good way. The compassionate, often maternal nature of the empath makes them perfect targets for the narc who knows that his or her empath will forgive them, make excuses for them and keep giving them another chance. Empaths see the best in people and the narcissist has shown them the very best in the early "love bombing" phase of the relationship. So, the empaths keep waiting for that potential to manifest again even though it never comes – or only comes in increasingly short busts before the cruel manipulator returns.

The empath seeks harmony, whereas the narcissist gets off on discord. What a recipe for disaster! The empath is downtrodden and treated like a doormat, whilst the narc creates more and more chaos, leaving the empath confused as to where they stand. Narcissists like Tom have no empathy and don't care about how others feel, whereas empaths like me are extremely sensitive. If we're not careful, we can become like an emotional sponge that sucks up everyone's negativity.

It's a toxic partnership. Either consciously or unconsciously, the narcissist seeks out an empath as they will be able to extract maximum use out of them. A person with mature, healthy boundaries would kick the narc out at the first sign of this bullying, controlling behaviour. So why do we put up with it? Often empaths don't have healthy boundaries because they have been abused in childhood, either physically or emotionally. In my case, with all the bullying and the rape, it was both.

Narcissists manipulate empaths by stringing them along with hope now and again – another powerful method of manipulation which I now know as "intermittent reinforcement." This is when a reward for instance Kindness, or punishment such as violence, is received for various actions, without any clear pattern. This keeps the empath trying to do things in the "right way", hoping to bring back their once-loving partner.

Tom's erratic behaviour kept me focused on my personality flaws, wondering what I needed to change to make him happy rather than blaming him. Every once in a while, when I said enough was enough, Tom would apologise, say he loved me and promise never do it again; a common technique narcs use to reel their partner back in, like a willing fish. It worked every time. Like most empaths, I was too forgiving; I chose to believe that Tom could and would change. Sometimes he was even on best behaviour for a while and I saw Nice Tom again. But he never followed through on his promises and before long, Nasty Tom was back.

This push and pull relationship forms what's known as a "trauma bond" between the victim and abuser, which makes it feel almost impossible to leave. To the horror of all my friends and family, I stayed with Tom for another year. In the end, I was seeking help from counsellors just to get strong enough to cope with him. Whenever I tried to break up with him, he would appear outside my house, apologise, and we would go around the whole destructive cycle again.

Then, nine months later, things started to change. I didn't hear from him as much; he'd say he wanted to meet up then wouldn't turn up. After everything I'd been through, you'd think I'd be pleased. But he had been so full on for the previous two years, that this pulling away hurt me. I was so deflated by all the trauma, I was a shell of my former self and felt like I couldn't cope without him. Now I realise that this is another common stage of the narcissist/empath pattern – the discard.

Empaths are so desperate to fix things, they will rarely leave a relationship willingly, but after the narcissist has sucked the empath dry, the narc will often find someone else to feed off, a new "narcissistic supply". Tom fitted the archetype perfectly. It was only when he found somebody else that he finally broke away. Although I didn't know it was happening at the time, I would come to find out that he had slept with everyone, including my friend whose kid's party I had met him at! And she broke up with him because he cheated on her too!

Looking back, I could have guessed that he was cheating on me. Once, when I was picking up his children from his house, I got to speak to his ex-wife. While they were married, they had a party at their house one night. She popped upstairs to check on the kids and, when she came back down, Tom was snogging her friend. Apparently, he shrugged and said, "Oh, it just happened." What kind of excuse is that?

She had a scar on her face too where Tom had chucked some car keys at her and once, he even threw a computer across the room, making their young son scream. She revealed that she had also had to phone the police on him because he had been so aggressive, which is why she didn't allow him to see their daughter. Of course, when I confronted Tom about it, he made out that she was just angry with him because he left her.

I let it go and things went back to normal – if that's what you can call it. Then, a few weeks later, we were playing around in the bedroom, but I could tell that he was in a mood. He had a shower, then when he got out, he whipped me really hard with the towel. It bought tears to my eyes.

"What the hell did you do that for?" I yelled.

I was so shocked that I grabbed my dressing gown and did it back to him. I accidentally hit him quite hard in the balls; he bent over double and groaned.

"Sorry," I gasped. "Are you okay?"

I felt terrible. I didn't mean to actually hurt him, I just don't know my own strength sometimes.

But Tom was furious. He got up and punched me hard in the throat. It knocked me to the floor; blood pouring from my nose, the carpet was covered in it. I told him to leave and not come back then took myself to A&E. My oesophagus swelled up so much that I couldn't swallow for three weeks and I couldn't eat. Thank God this didn't happen in front of the kids; they were with their dad at the time. I always made sure they were away when Tom came around just in case. I'd never put my kids through any of that. Looking back, I wonder why I thought it was okay to put myself through it?

After that, everything went quiet. I had no contact from Tom at all. Three days later, it was his birthday. We were still friends on Facebook, where I saw that he changed his status to "in a relationship." Then he posted lots of pictures of him with this new woman; it looked like they had been together for months. I was absolutely gutted. It was like someone had winded me. How could he do this? He didn't even have the decency to tell me. But, on the other hand, it was as if the chains had been broken from me. *Oh my God, I thought, it's finally over. At last, I'm free!*

From that moment on, I vowed that I would never let a man treat me like that again. I had a new direction; instead of giving my energy to a man, I would focus on myself and my family. Now it was just me and the kids, facing the world. Instead of looking after a guy, I would prioritise my own well-being. This was the start of me breaking the cycle of abuse and learning how to set healthy boundaries. For empaths, setting boundaries can feel harsh. But we have to find the strength to say "no," so we can protect ourselves from people taking advantage of us. Not everybody needs to be in our lives; some others might not be healthy for us, and we need to be able to let them go.

Although it was difficult at the time to be discarded, now I give thanks that Tom disappeared from my life. If I was still with him, I wouldn't be where I am today. I might even be dead. Yes, I was upset and crying at first. But when the tears dried, I realised that I was lucky to be out of it. After seeing Tom on Facebook with another woman, I decided to take time out from social media. I took a step back from concentrating on other people. I could never be free if I had too much drama in my life, so I learnt to cut out everything else and focus on myself.

I decided that I needed to be physically stronger, so that I could defend myself if I was ever in this kind of situation again. When I did modelling, I had been a " Ring Girl", walking around the boxing ring, holding up the board. I loved it, not just because of being on stage, but also because I got to watch people box. I fell in love with the fighting industry. It's not just a brawl, like some people think, it's a real art with clever technique and skill. I like watching the way people move and how they handle themselves, and there's nothing sexier than a man who can fight. Maybe, unconsciously, I was craving someone to protect me. But now I thought, *why can't I be my own protector?*

One fighter that I knew had a little gym near me that did MMA – Mixed Martial Arts. So, I started training with him and got to spa with all the lads there, who were amazing. Everyone was so supportive and respectful of everyone else, it was great. There was only one other woman there, who was very tall. The first time I had to pin her down, she was shocked that she couldn't get out of my hold.

"For a teeny, tiny thing, you're bloody strong," she gasped. "You might be little but you're tough!"

Her saying this gave me so much confidence. I felt powerful and not like a weak, little victim anymore. Learning to fight made me fee like I was taking back my power. I would recommend it to any woman of any age.

But, of course, I couldn't just focus on external strength; I had to toughen up on the inside too. It was time to take a good, hard look in the mirror. I had been around men that had treated me badly for so many years, it had knocked my self-esteem into the dirt. *Why are you letting them do it?* I asked myself. *Why don't you look after yourself?* When you've always had abusive relationships, you often don't even realise that there's anything wrong.

As I examined my life, I could see my pattern; instead of taking time to be on my own and really find myself, I entered into a co-dependent relationship. From now on, I had to stay more conscious and take responsibility for myself. I realised that I needed to cut away from people with lots of issues and find others that want to succeed and wouldn't hold me back.

There are men out there that will love you for you, I told myself. But until you find one that is really as good as he says he is, then it's the single life for you!

What a relief that was. Looking back, I saw the similarities between all the men I had been with since my teenage years. I realised that it had taken me a long time to get over my heartbreak from Rob, my first love. Funnily enough, around the time I broke up with Tom, Rob got back in touch with me. He sent me a message on Facebook, and I replied. It made me feel a bit unhappy, but I was stronger now and could cope with talking to him again.

Rob told me that he was still with the girl from school and lived in the same place with their kids. I realised that if I had stayed with him, I wouldn't have liked my life. He never wanted to travel and had no passion or ambitions. It was like the universe was telling me that what happened to me, however hard, was meant to be. I just had to learn it for myself. You have to take the positives from everything that happens in life. Ultimately, this experience with Tom and all my other exes taught me some very valuable – if painful – lessons. They'd pushed me to make the changes that I needed and gave me the drive to succeed.

It was not long after the break-up with Tom, around Christmas time, that the movie *Charlie's Angels* came on TV; that fateful day that I decided to change my destiny. From this moment forth, I vowed to keep all the drama in my life on the screen!

THE ROLLERCOASTER

The pilot for the reality TV show about footballers that I presented was sent out to production companies and TV channels all over town. Every day, I'd nervously check to see if I'd received a message with news. The director kept saying it was coming any minute now and I was sure that my career was about to take off big time.

Unfortunately, that message never came, and the show never did get picked up. It didn't take off because there were too many reality shows at the time. And so that was the end of that. I was absolutely gutted; I'd built up all my hopes and really believed that this project was going to happen. I didn't yet realise how dangerous it is to do that in this business.

I was sacrificing everything for my career and my children. Other people I knew were partying, going out and getting drunk on the weekends. I was always the one that stayed into study and research what I needed to do. I assumed that because I was putting in so much hard work, determination and passion, I would quickly see results. But every time I turned a corner and thought I was getting somewhere, another door slammed in my face.

In addition to *Star Now*, I put my profile up on *Mandy.com*, a website that showcases actors to casting directors, directors and producers – for a fee, of course. Once again, I kept getting offered roles, but then nothing would come of it. It was always the same pattern.

"You're perfect for this," they'd coo. "Can you put something on camera?"

Often the message would come in at the last minute too, so I'd have to cancel all my plans to make sure I was ready for the deadline.

I'd spend hours getting all dressed up and finding the right monologue. I'd film myself performing it, doing countless takes until I'd really nailed the emotion.

"Wow, that's great," they'd reply after watching it. "We'll get back to you soon."

I'd get really excited about the project and start dreaming about the shoot. But then I would never hear from them again!

It was very common to not even be told that you hadn't got the job, let alone why not. My acting teacher, the casting director from Manchester, had warned us about this.

"Even if you do auditions but don't get picked, it's not something you're doing wrong," she'd explained. "Often the casting directors want something so specific, you just don't look the part for them."

She was trying to prepare us for the inevitable disappointment that comes with being an actor, presenter or model.

"This is what you have to get into your head," she'd insist. "It's not that you're not good. You're just not right for this role."

As I fruitlessly applied for job after job, I tried to remind myself of her words.

Sometimes they even cast someone else in a role that they'd already declared you were perfect for. More often than not, the whole project didn't go ahead at all. I came to realise that I couldn't believe anything anyone said – so much of it was just hype and PR. You could only believe it was actually happening when the money was in the bank. And this doesn't just happen with actors. One producer told me that he'd even filmed shows with big name talent, only for the TV networks to cancel them at the last minute because it didn't fit in with their programming schedule.

"I learnt the hard way," he muttered, bitterly. "Now, I only believe it's really happening when I see my show up on the TV screen!"

The industry put me on a constant emotional rollercoaster and was very stressful. One minute, I was on a high because I felt that it was all going to work out and I was going to make it. The next, I plummeted to rock bottom because it all seemed hopeless after all. If you work in a bank or you're a lawyer or doctor, there is usually a clear career progression. Your status and income gradually improve as you gain more experience. Not so with showbiz, there really is no business like it.

It was so hard because on the one hand, you had to sustain the passion and excitement to keep going for jobs and putting yourself out there. But, on the other, you couldn't get too attached to the outcome because so often things didn't pan out. It's a very tough world to break into. It's hard enough if you come from a famous acting family, graduate from a top drama school or have lots of money behind you. But if you're coming from nowhere, it's a real struggle.

I felt like I was doing everything I could to chase my dreams and better my children's future. But sometimes it felt like a constant battle, and I feared that I was never going to get anywhere. I began to worry that I had started too late. I researched the age that some of my favourite actors had made it. A lot of the big names were child stars like Drew Barrymore, who starred in the blockbuster *ET* aged seven, and Jodie Foster, who began her professional career as a child model when she was three. By twelve, she was starring in *Taxi Driver* and nominated for an Oscar!

I was amazed to find out how many household names began their careers in childhood. Natalie Portman was eleven when she starred in *Léon: The Professional (1994)* and is still a star today. Leonardo Di Caprio appeared in *Romper Room* at the age of five. Ryan Gosling was barely a teenager when he was in *The All New Mickey Mouse Club* in 1993. Jake Gyllenhaal acted in his first film age eleven; he also came from an acting family and appeared in films with his sister, directed by their dad. Likewise, Keira Knightly was the child of a playwright and actor, who got her start in a British TV series at three years old. Scarlett Johansson was ten when she appeared in Rob Reiner's film *North*. Reece Witherspoon made her acting debut in *The Man in the Moon (1991)* at fourteen.

Reading all this made my heart sink. It was demoralising, especially as I knew that the business was particularly hard for women, where it was so much about youth and beauty. Actresses that I met at auditions whispered about "the rush to make it before you're thirty." Well, I had already reached that grand old age. Surely it was too late for me?

Before I spiralled into a depression, I decided that I needed to take a break and get myself in hand. I had to get my thought process together and get strong. I started to watch female motivational speakers and talks by powerful women. I had my best girlfriends around for a pow wow; they were so positive and encouraging. Karen and Tracey really helped me – they were my Laura's Angels!

I also read lots of books on mindfulness and positive thinking. One had a quote I loved by Marcus Aurelius, a Stoic philosopher, who was the Emperor of Rome from 161 to 180 AD.

"The object of life is not to be on the side of the majority, but to escape finding oneself in the ranks of the insane."

I could certainly relate to that!

There was one particular book that had a huge influence on me. One day, I was in Starbucks having a coffee, when there was a guy next to me reading *The Secret*. We started chatting and he told me that I should have a look at it. Written in 2006, *The Secret* is a self-help book by Rhonda Byrne. It's all about the Law of Attraction and claims that your thoughts can change your life; if you think about a certain thing as if you already have it then you can draw it towards you. *The Secret* certainly changed the author's life; the book sold more than thirty-five million copies worldwide and been translated into fifty languages.

I hadn't even heard of the book back then, but my new friend said it had changed his whole life. Back in his twenties, he was a soldier and didn't have any money. Someone told him about the documentary *The Secret* and he watched it then got the book, which was based on the film. Ever since, he read it every day and could even recite parts from it. He was in his forties now and a millionaire that drove a Bentley!

"That's interesting," I said, politely.

But deep down, I was thinking it seemed like a load of shit! You couldn't just manifest things with your thoughts, could you? That was a pipe dream, surely. But I said I'd give it a try. I downloaded the audio book and listened to it whilst on a bike ride in the mountains. The man advised me to try to manifest something so specific that it wouldn't even seem possible. I thought it would be really nice if someone treated me for once, rather than it just being me sorting the kids out all the time. It would be nice to get something back for a change.

When I got back from the mountains, there was a parcel at the door for me. *That's weird,* I thought, *I haven't ordered anything.* I opened it up and it was the biggest box of posh chocolates that I'd ever seen. My friend from London had sent it to me to cheer me up.

I couldn't believe my eyes. Okay, maybe this stuff really works.

I listened to the book again. *Everyone's the same in this world,* I thought. *So how come some have achieved what they wanted to, and I haven't? Let's figure this out.* I could hear all the reasons that my mind was saying was why I couldn't make it, like, "Oh, I can't, I have five kids."

"Then get a nanny," I said to myself. "Just do it, find a way!"

I kept listening to the book until it really changed my outlook. I wasn't going to believe my own limitations anymore – that was just a negative story I told myself. It was time for that story to change. In the end, I felt so excited. *I'm going to make it,* I told myself, *I know I will be successful.*

I wanted to help people and be an actress and stuntwoman – why couldn't I do it all?

I used to be a strong person, I thought. *I can be again.* I pushed all the concerns that I had left it too late out of my mind. *Okay, I'm thirty now, but so what? Who cares about age?* I truly believed that if you really focus on what you want to do, you can do it. I knew that I was determined enough, especially now that I didn't have any abusive men dragging me down.

Sure, many actors did start young but lots of stars got their break later in life. Jon Hamm spent years starring in minor roles and almost gave it all up, until he landed the lead role in the hit TV show *Mad Men*. Viola Davis, the Oscar nominated actress from *The Help*, didn't graduate from drama school until she was nearly thirty. Jessica Chastain had trouble getting parts until she was thirty-four because of her red hair. Morgan Freeman was also thirty-four when he made his TV debut. Harrison Ford was a full-time carpenter until he was thirty-five. Ken Jeong from *The Hangover* was a doctor until he was forty. Samuel L Jackson's first big role was in *Pulp Fiction* age 45.

Okay, so it wasn't going to be easy. But if they could do it, so could I. Of course, it would have been good to have come to this realisation a bit younger, but I would get there in the end.

"We can do anything we want," I declared to the universe. "From now on, I'm going to manifest my dreams!"

BACK TO SCHOOL

Now I was single, I had more time and energy to give to my kids and they started to thrive. Our bond, which had always been deep, grew stronger than ever. We've always been big on family time but now us Super Six took it to another level. We always ate breakfast and dinner together around the table, just talking with no TV or other distractions, and had plenty of days out walking, swimming or horse riding. My kids were my best friends.

Unlike my ex's, the children were totally supportive of my dreams.

"Mummy wants to be an actress," they boasted to anyone who would listen. "And we're going to help her."

They shared my passion for entertaining and we performed little family shows for ourselves, which was great fun. Of course, I'm biased but I think my brood are a talented bunch. Shannon is an excellent dancer, Blake can do backflips and Maliki can really belt out a tune. They're all really sporty too, like their mum. At the weekend, we'd push the furniture back and spend hours together in the living room doing acrobatics and stunts. They were some of the best times of my life.

Balancing work and the family could be challenging though. I was working as a cleaner in local houses at the time, which was handy because I could fit it in around the children, my stunt training and going to auditions. Money was pretty tight – I got no child support from either father because they said they couldn't afford it. So, I thought that I had to find something to fall back on in case I never broke through in showbusiness. Yes, I was thinking positively now but I was also realistic; I had five kids to provide for, after all.

I considered what other opportunities were open to me. Even though I had given up my job as a nurse, I still enjoyed helping people. Plus reading *The Secret* and all those self-help books had got me interested in how the mind works. I decided that, if I studied psychology, I could become a psychiatrist or counsellor. I have always been fascinated by the way people think and I knew psychology would be good research for my acting career. So, it was a win-win situation all round.

I signed up to the BA in psychology at Wrexham University. I had left school at fifteen with no qualifications, so this was a big deal for me. I was not confident on any level about my academic prowess, but I knew this was just another self-imposed limitation that I had to bust through. I enrolled to start in September of that year. Because I didn't have any qualifications, I had to take the first year as a foundation course and repeat my English and Maths GCSEs, then I could swap onto the BA. This meant that the course would take four years in total. It seemed like a big-time commitment, but a good foundation for the future, so I decided to take the plunge.

The fees were expensive, but I secured a student loan to cover them. I had to go into the university three days a week. I was still working sixteen hours a week cleaning, but I could fit in the classes around it. I was nervous to go back into education as school had not been a happy period in my life. But I drew on everything I had learnt from the motivations speakers and built up my confidence. *It will be different this time around,* I told myself. *This is a new start for me.*

Now, I was going back to school as a mature woman. *I won't let things get to me this time,* I told myself. *Everyone's an adult so no one will pick on anyone.* This was a new chance for me to get on with my life. I was really excited and looking forward to making new friends with similar interests. *It's going to be easy and fun!*

September came and the first term began. At first, it was tough being back in an educational institution and felt quite daunting. But the classes were interesting, and I soon got stuck in. All the psychology books that I was reading really helped with my acting. The science of how the mind worked was excellent for getting into characters' heads. So, the course started well; I seemed to make friends quickly and everything seemed fine.

Then, all of a sudden, everything changed. The girls who had been so nice saw on my Facebook page all the modelling and acting that I had done. They wanted to do some too and asked me to help them, so I talked through how the business works and sent them the details of some agencies. However, they never followed through on them, so it never came to anything. After that, their behaviour towards me turned. They wouldn't talk to me and isolated me from all the tasks. On the rare occasions that I was late after having dropped the kids off at school, they would bad mouth me behind my back to the rest of the class. One girl stood up for me and told them to stop, but they wouldn't listen to her.

I couldn't believe it; here I was back at school being bullied by girls who were at least a decade younger than me, for no reason at all. What the hell was going on? I thought about the Law of Attraction; had I drawn this experience to myself because it was what had happened to me at school before? At first, they made me feel really small. But then I had an epiphany. Yes, this was happening again, but I didn't have to react in the same way. That was my choice. *This isn't the be-and-end-all of my life*, I thought. *So what if they are bullying you? Does it really matter if they slag me off?*

When you're young, you think it's the end of the world if the other girls don't like you. But when you grow up, you come to understand that you're not going to be everyone's cup of tea.

The more you realise this, the freer you are. Going to university was a small part of my life; the rest of the time, my energy was devoted to my children and my career. As long as my kids were happy and loved, that was all that counted. I focused all my positive energy on more important things and didn't let the bullying affect me anymore.

I had been crippled by other people's judgements all my life. Now I didn't care so much what others thought of me. I had become more thick-skinned; whatever life threw at me, I could handle it. It almost seemed as if the universe was giving me a test by playing out the same circumstances as in my childhood. This was my opportunity to act differently; the chance to prove to myself that I had changed and was no longer that timid, little victim of my youth.

This experience gave me closure on my past and put a stop to those negative patterns. In a way, I had to thank these girls for playing out this drama so that I could give the story a different ending this time. Instead of letting myself go into a negative spiral, taking it all to heart and maybe even running away like when I was fifteen, I confronted the issue headlong.

One day, before the lessons started, I addressed the whole class.

"Does anyone have any problems with me?" I asked, ensuring that I made eye contact with all the bullies. "Can we address this please?" I continued but they just lowered their heads in shame. "If there's any issues, let's discuss it now, or you can come and see me, and we can chat one to one. If not, let's just get on with the course."

No one ever came to see me and nothing more was ever said after that. No one bullied me again. When they knew it wasn't affecting me, they moved on to someone else.

After confronting this issue, I felt a huge surge of energy and a rush of euphoria, as you do when you overcome any fear. I was proud of myself for changing my patterns. I wasn't going to take on anyone's shit anymore. From that moment onwards, I felt liberated. I don't care if others find me attractive and likeable or not. I'm just me. When you get older different things matter. "Don't sweat the small stuff," as the self-help guru Richard Carlson once said. Once you let go of the small things, the big things can really start to happen.

Until you can let go of what other people think of you, you can't truly be free. Unfortunately, there will always be haters. It's sad fact of this world; look at all the internet trolls out there. Okay, so people might try and tear you down, but you have to learn to love yourself as you are. That was the hardest lesson I had to learn. You take so much shit then one day, you wake up and think, *why am I letting this affect me?* A different part of your mind takes over from the small, insecure child within. *Will I ever even see these people again?* You realise. My family love me for who I am, and I have a small group of friends that will stand by me no matter what. *So, at the end of the day, does anyone else count?* To which the answer is a resounding NO!

CUNNING STUNTS

It was time for me to take my career to the next level and join the number one casting database in the country, Spotlight. Founded in 1927, all the performers are on there – from fresh-faced newbies just out of drama school to Oscar-winning stars of stage and screen. When it first started, Spotlight was just a slim volume with a few actors' photographs. Nowadays, it runs into many volumes and over 70,000 performers use it to showcase themselves. It's the actor's bible!

I knew I had to be in Spotlight to expand my profile, but there was just one catch; I didn't have the professional experience to get in. They didn't count credits in adverts or extra work; it had to be proper speaking roles in film, TV or theatre. One of the ways to get around this was if you had a degree in TV, drama or theatre. I found out that my university in Wrexham had a course that qualified and went to the library to read up about it. It sounded so good that I ran straight over to the film and TV department and one of the tutors gave me a guided tour. He led me through the studio, passing students acting and filming, then I read some of their scripts. *Wow!* I thought, *I love this. This is definitely where I should be.*

Because of my TV experience, they offered me a place to start in Level Two, so I only had to do two more years. Now I just had to tell my psychology teachers that it would be better for my career to switch courses. Fortunately, they were very understanding. They saw the potential I had with acting and told me to go for it. In fact, they really helped me. I felt that I could talk to them about anything. Even to this day, if things get too much, I can still go back and see them. I've still got a diploma in psychology. I believe that everything happens for a reason so maybe the psychology was meant to make me the actor I am today.

I had to wait until September to start the new course so, for the time being, I focused on my stunt training. I was practising all the activities from the stunt register possible. I did something every day of the week; swimming, gymnastics, horse riding, martial arts, rock climbing … whatever I could cram in. But stunt training is a lonely place to be. It's constant hard work and there's no-one else around so you have to really push yourself.

I decided to look for some peers to help keep me motivated and provide mutual support. On Facebook, I found a group of stuntmen around the UK that were already on the register. We went on some trips together to practise different stunts, especially jumping as you can't train for that indoors; you have to jump into water.

I had always loved jumping. When I was into swimming as a child, I used to do high dives. I always did some in my favourite place Anglesey too, as there are lots of cliff jumps there. It can be risky though, so you have to be careful. Before you jump, you check the depth of the water by throwing a stone in to see how far it sinks. Then you do some small jumps into the river or sea to depth check; if it's too shallow, you could kill yourself when you leap from higher up. You also have to throw a stone to break the water before you jump because if the water is too flat, it's like hitting concrete.

Technique is so important with jumping. You want to land feet first, ideally with pointed toes; it can shatter your spine if you land with flat feet. You need to avoid falling back as you might hit your head when you land. You don't want to fall forward either so, as tempting as it might be, never look down while you jump.

The biggest threat in cliff diving is the speed. When you're falling, speed builds quickly; even when you're jumping twenty feet, you can have a speed of up to twenty-five miles an hour when you hit the water. That can break your bones and compress your spine. From sixty foot, you could easily die because that's equal to sixty miles an hour. Imagine the damage you can do if you hit the water as fast as that.

People don't realise how dangerous jumping is. But no matter how nervous you are, it's important to keep your body loose when jumping and not to tense up. Once you commit to the jump, you have to go for it. You can't chicken out as that can make it worse; you might tense your body or change your position and land wrongly. Make sure that you breathe as you're going down then take another breath when you're about to hit the water – don't hold your breath. Once, I jumped off a sixty-foot cliff and I held my breath at the top. That was a big mistake because, by the time I'd gone under water and come up again, I could have drowned.

It's serious stuff so you've got to know your limits. However, when it goes well, jumping is one of the biggest kicks in the world. You're hyper aware when you're going down and you have an amazing sense of freedom, like you're flying through the air. It's like no other feeling in the world. It's so euphoric – partly because you are flirting with danger. When you come up in the water, you think, *Thank God, I'm okay, I've made it this time.* It's the most alive you've ever felt in your life.

It was such fun to have this group of like-minded, new friends to go jumping with. However, it was mostly lads, who all took the piss out of us women.

"You're girls, you can't do what we do," they sneered.

Even the ones that didn't say anything like that were still quite sexist deep down. They didn't really care what you could do – they just wanted to go to bed with you.

"You're really attractive," they'd coo. "If you sleep with me, I'll get you on location for this job."

But I wasn't tempted. I've never slept with anyone for a role, nor would I.

For our first trip, we went to some local cliffs where you could do jumping then we went on to some fantastic locations with insane jumps like Blue Lagoon in South Wales. Next, we went to Killiecrankie in Scotland, located on the River Garry. The scenery is absolutely stunning up there and there's place with a one-hundred-foot bridge where you can jump straight into water.

When we arrived, we started by practising with some little jumps off the rocks. It was a sunny day, but the water was still absolutely freezing. The whole time, we were all looking up at the bridge and considering the big drop.

"Who's going to do it?" one guy asked.

"I will!" I replied.

All the lads started giggling.

"Come on then," the guy said. "Let's challenge each other."

So, we all went up to the bridge. We did the test and jumped down lower, so we knew the height was okay and there was plenty of depth for it to be safe.

The lads were taking the piss out of each other, almost acting as if I wasn't there.

"Go on, you go," one said.

"Wait a minute, let me get my breath," another replied then turned to his mate and asked, "What about you?"

They were all acting as if they were totally fine with it. But none of them wanted to go first.

So, I decided to take the lead.

"I'll do it," I announced.

They just burst out laughing at that.

"No, you won't," they declared, thinking I was joking. I was only a girl after all.

To show I meant what I said, I climbed over the rails. As I hauled myself over the cold metal bars, I felt bubbles of excitement and nerves churn up in my gut. Of course, we had done things like this before, so I knew I was going to be alright, but it was still very challenging. I stayed there hanging over the safety bars for a few moments, looking down at the drop below. As I did, my legs wobbled and my stomach dropped. *Shit, this was high!*

"You can come back now," the guys said. "You don't have to go through with this."

But they didn't know me very well. I'm a woman of my word.

"Bye," I said and jumped off the edge.

Once I had done the jump, they had to as well; they couldn't be shown up, especially not by a woman. One of the guys hadn't done many jumps, so, as he fell, he looked down; he was going at a fast pace, and the water hit him so hard that he ended up with two black eyes. Poor thing. That's why training is so important – you have to know the correct way of doing things, otherwise you can do yourself serious damage.

After I did the jump, I was treated differently and got a new-found respect from the guys. This was a clear sign that they were seeing me differently – not just as a big breasted blonde! From then on, they started taking me more seriously. They backed off me too and stopped flirting with me. Some even apologised.

"We've messed up," they said. "We shouldn't be treating you like this, trying to hit on to you all the time. You're one of us now."

The day after the jump, we climbed The Cuillins, the Rocky Mountains which dominate the landscape on the Isle of Skye. The iconic Black Cuillin ridge is Britain's most challenging mountain range, over 11 kilometres long and above 3,000 feet in places. The highest point is Sgurr Alasdair at 3,254.59 feet.

I love mountain climbing – I can do it all day. But the weather can be very unpredictable up there. It was quite dangerous when we tackled it because it was thick fog and we couldn't see very far in front of us. Through the gloom, we spotted another group of rock climbers, who told us that the easiest route was to go around the edge to the other part of the mountain. But, when we did, there was a sheer drop to your death; we only just managed to see it in time. They had given us the wrong directions; we were lucky we didn't slide off the edge!

Later on, the weather had cleared but I had a little accident. I didn't quite have a good grip on the rock when I made the move. One of the lads said, "You'll be fine doing this," but it didn't feel right. I reached up for the rock, but I didn't manage to make the grip. My foot fell out of the bottom hole and I couldn't get it back in quick enough. It's a metre's drop between carabiners, the metal climbing loops you put your rope through. I ended up falling off the rock and swinging from one carabiner to another on the side of the mountain. I felt like a right fool!

In this game, it's so dangerous not think about things thoroughly, no matter what anyone says to you. If you know or even think you haven't got hold, don't do it. I've come to learn that I should always trust my gut instincts. Still, despite – or maybe because of – all the potential danger, that trip gave me bug to do more. And more and more. When I got home, I resumed my training with a new passion. I was pushing myself all the time.

However, it was all taking a toll on my body. I was driving myself to the point of exhaustion, but I was so determined, I couldn't slow down. I had been working my whole life for this; I wasn't letting anything stop me now. Physically, I was really suffering but it's amazing what your body can do when your mind is so focused. Unfortunately, I didn't take my own well-being into consideration. So maybe it's no surprise that something had to give.

BREAK A LEG

All this training started to pay off and I was offered an exciting new job – a stunt role in the third *Transformers* film. We were set to film in Detroit in September, just before I went back to university to start my new course. I was so thrilled about this opportunity. *Finally, my career's taking off,* I thought. *I'm really getting noticed now.*

Once again, I spoke too soon. About three weeks before the shoot, I was in my local gymnasium doing trampoline training with some friends and our coach. We were practising how to fall and land, freefalling and back flips. I'd been practising my triple flip. I'd just managed to do it for the first time and was dead excited. I tried it again and bounced on the trampoline. I soared up into the air, but, as I came down, my leg locked, and my ankle twisted all the way around.

I broke my leg in three places; I knew it straight away. I felt each and every snap.

"I've just broken my leg," I told my friends, quite casually.

Maybe it was the way I said it, but nobody believed me.

"No, you haven't," they laughed. "It's fine."

"Yes, I have," I protested.

They thought I was making it up and started teasing me for being melodramatic.

"Come on, Laura, get up!"

But I was absolutely sure what had happened.

"I can't walk on it because I don't want to create more damage."

When I tried to stand up, they soon realised that I wasn't joking. They helped me hobble to the car. None of them had a driving license so I had to drive myself to hospital.

When I told the nurse what had happened, they got me straight in and laid me out on a table to look me over. My friends stayed with me to check that I was okay. The nurse sent me for an X-ray and confirmed that, sure enough, I had broken it in three places. So they wrapped it up and I had to drive myself home. In the end, they had to put a metal plate in my leg and pins in my ankle.

Of course, I couldn't do the stunt job. I was so upset; it felt like the end of the world. I was so looking forward to it. Yet again, I had been stopped in my tracks – quite literally this time. In the theatre, when you go on stage, you're never wished "good luck", which paradoxically is considered bad luck! Instead, you're told to, "Break a leg!" The term dates back to Shakespeare's time, when to "break a leg" meant to bow by bending at the knee when receiving applause, so it was a good thing. Seems I took the expression a bit too literally!

In all, my broken leg put me out for three months. I wasn't a happy bunny at all. But it's at times like these that you see who your true friends are. Everyone was really there for me. My best friend Jack, the world title martial artist and kick boxer, supported me throughout the whole thing. He helped with the kids, took them to school and cooked them dinner. He did the housework too as he knew I liked a clean home. He did everything that I couldn't do, all the time telling me jokes to cheer me up. He was my absolute rock.

My parents came up to help me too. Mum bought me loads of food and prepared dishes to put in the freezer. She did everything she could to make life easier for me and the children. Of course, my folks weren't too impressed by my stunt training.

"We worry about you," Mum cried. "You could end up killing yourself!"

They are the type of people that are nervous of everything; they're not adrenaline junkies like me. They've just had your typical working jobs all their lives and aren't adventurous. None of my family are. But I always craved adventure.

Although my folks kept trying to put me off becoming a stunt woman, when they saw how determined I was, they accepted it – broken leg and all.

"You've always gone for what you wanted in life," Dad said, "We might not like what you're doing but we'll always support you."

In September, I finally started my new TV and drama course at Wrexham university – on crutches, with my foot in plaster and a big, plastic boot. Not the best start; I couldn't even be in the first production because of my leg. But, at least, I got to watch and do some directing. It was quite interesting to see the way people interacted. The drama students were very different from those doing psychology; a lot of them were quite self-important and competitive, always trying to outdo one another.

For the Christmas show, we had to devise a theatre piece. I cast four actors, but they weren't very professional and wouldn't turn up for rehearsals or learn their lines. In the end, they did pull through and it was okay, but it was difficult to deal with that, when you're really focused and want to get the job done. I remember watching all these drama queens and thinking, *how are you going to make it?* You have to focus on set and work as part of a team. You can't waltz around being a prima donna – not until you're a big star anyway!

At the end of the course, for my dissertation, I created a forty-five-minute stunt show. I was really excited; this was my chance to show off all of the skills I'd been learning over the last few years. The final performance featured Acro-yoga routines, incorporating moves from yoga and acrobatics, Arial hoop, a couple of fight scenes, and a big UV light show. I called upon all my stunt friends and got them involved. They pulled through for me too, bless them, and I ended up getting a first for my degree.

Now I had finished university, I had to weigh up my options. I thought about moving to London, where there were more castings and opportunities in the industry. But my kids were settled in Wrexham, so I decided to stay there; London was only a two-hour train journey away, after all. I was still thinking long term about me and the kids, *if this doesn't work, what will I do as a back-up?* So I decided to do a PGCE, which would qualify me to become a professional teacher in film, TV and drama. I loved helping others with their acting, almost as much as I loved doing it myself.

But for now, it was summer and time for a family holiday. Every year, I took the children to Anglesey – it's my favourite place in the UK. Every year, they have an agricultural show there, which we adore. You can feed the cows and goats, see horses show jumping, and there are competitions to find the fastest sheep shearer. It's proper country fun!

At that year's show, I noticed they had an area for some ladies who were competing in the Wales Strongest Woman contest. I imagined that strong women had to be huge but in fact, they were all my size. We were on one side of the fence, watching them lift weights. *I'm pretty strong,* I thought. *I bet I can do that.*

I called over the guy to ask him for more information.

"Come around and have a look at the equipment," he said. "You can give it a go."

First, I tried the deadlifting bar. It was 120 Kg and I lifted it easily, which made me feel quite euphoric.

"Wow, this is amazing," I announced. "I love this."

I could tell the guy was impressed.

"You're strong," he declared. "Very strong."

Next, there was a 15 kg weight, shaped like the Welsh dragon. You had to raise it up and hold it in front of your face for as long as possible.

So I lifted it, and again, felt super comfortable. The kids were very excited too.

"Wow, Mum, that's amazing," they cried in awe.

The guy came back over, and we had a chat. His name was Bruce and it turned out that he lived just ten minutes down the road from me.

"Well, if you're local, maybe you can train me to compete for Wales's Strongest Woman?" I asked.

Bruce couldn't believe his ears. He laughed for a second and then nodded.

"Sure thing."

He took my number and said we could start training straight away. When I left the fair, I was full of anticipation. Here was a new adventure, something I would have never imagined that I would do.

WALES' STRONGEST WOMAN

On the first day of training, I was buzzing. I had bought a sporty, new top for the occasion, made of Lycra with a zip all the way up the chest. When I got to Bruce's home, I had the pleasure of meeting his wife; they were a really nice family. Then the coach led me through to a unit at the back of their house, which he had built for training. There were all kinds of apparatus in there; weights, tyres, bars, you name it. He even had one of those cars with the middle taken out so you could get under and lift it up like I'd seen on strong man shows on TV. *Wow, this is so exciting*, I thought. I was raring to go.

Bruce explained what was going to happen and told me a little more about the competition. It turned out that, despite their size, all the ladies competing have to lift the same weight. It seemed a bit unfair because I'm only 60kg, whilst some of the women I would be competing against would be over 100kg. You have classes for smaller girls, but to win the whole competition, you have to lift as much as the big girls. That's just the way it is.

For a moment, I felt down hearted. *I'm never going to lift what they can.* But then I thought back to all the stunt training that I'd done, and I knew I'd be capable, even if it took a lot of practise. *Right, I'm going to really get my teeth into this.*

"First, we're going to do a warm-up," Bruce announced.

So, I began jogging on the spot and stretching, doing some yoga positions. It's important to get your body completely warm before you start training otherwise you can pull a muscle and get serious injuries. I started to do some star jumps to get my heart pumping. But, as I moved, the zip on my new top burst open at the bottom then undid all the way up to the top. There I was, trying to be this strong woman and my boobs fell out. Talk about costume failure!

I was so embarrassed, but Bruce leant me one of his old T shirts to wear and we got on with the session. He wanted to see how much I could lift. We started with the 60kg deadlift, a loaded bar, which you raise up to the hips. You have to lock your knees for it to class as a proper lift.

I found that easy so then we went all the way up to 100kg, which was fine as well. Bruce looked a bit shocked.

"You're a strong little fucker, aren't ya?" he teased

I had to laugh. I know I'm not what you'd expect me to be like from the outside. With my blonde hair and babyface, I look like a dainty, little girl. But in reality, I'm not like that at all.

Bruce wanted to see how strong I really was. We went outside where he had a bar with tyres on each side; you had to lift it up to your chest then walk around in a circle holding it up for as long as you can. I managed to lift that with 100kg. Bruce was quite impressed, which psyched me up to do even more.

The training for World's Strongest Women is exhausting, a huge challenge for your body and mind. The weight of these bars is no joke. It's tough and you have to go through a lot of pain. Every time you're doing a lift, you focus deep on whoever or whatever has hurt you in the past then you channel all that energy into the lift. You put all your force in and go as far as you can with it. In a way, it's a bit like drawing on your emotional memory of previous experiences when you're acting, for example, if you have to cry in a scene, you remember a time that upset you. Of course, I've had five kids, so I know all about pain!

It's funny because, despite, or perhaps because of the pain, training is very addictive. Coming away after the first session, I was euphoric. I felt so high, like I was on drugs. I hadn't eaten the whole day either because I wasn't prepared. I was absolutely starving afterwards so I went to the butchers on the way home and bought the whole shop! I slept for about twelve hours that night. The next day, my legs and bum were killing me, and I could barely walk or sit down. But it was worth it, and I was looking forward to going back for more.

The next week, we got a bit deeper into the training. I was joined by a thirty-year-old guy called Mike. He was an excellent lifter and had come second in The Giants Live World's Strongest Man Tour on TV. There was also a mum of two kids called Jeanie. She had just started to train but was already really good. She was very pretty and petite, but super muscly.

I got chatting to Jeanie and she gave me some pointers. She was training for a bench press competition. Because she had that coming up, Bruce put more focus on her so Mike worked with me. One of Mike's strong points was dead lifts, so he helped me with that, to make sure I perfected my form. Although I was lifting 100kg, I wasn't doing it quite right; I was using my back instead of my legs. Mike explained that could cause problems, especially as the weights got heavier. If I wasn't careful, I could risk putting my back out or slipping a disk.

I loved training with Mike. It was really exciting having someone there who'd had so much experience and success in the Strong Man industry. He also had a very positive attitude. I soon realised that you can either be really aggressive or really happy when you're training and draw on either of these energies; it can go both ways. We've all seen those Strong Men on TV who roar with anger when they lift heavy weights. For myself, I really struggled to tap into that aggression. Instead, I found that, when I was happier, I able to lift far more; positivity was as important as physical strength.

Bruce told me that, in the next session, I was going to be training with all the girls I would be competing against in Wales's Strongest Woman. I was a little nervous about this – what if they were really aggressive or even bullied me? But the other girls weren't what I expected; they were all lovely. Every single one was encouraging; no-one put the others down. It was nothing like being at school or even university. Finally, I was in a learning environment, which was gentle, friendly and supportive – for a Strong Woman competition, where you would least expect it!

There were about ten other women in all, of all ages up to their fifties. Two were about my size but the rest were a good deal bigger in height and weight. One woman called Pat was in her forties. She was incredible; I would watch her in awe. Pat revealed that, when she was lifting weights, she pisses herself all the time. I thought she was joking at first but apparently, that's normal. She told me the heavier the weights are, the more women wee. All the strong women know about it, so they often wear panty liners. That threw me off because I kept thinking I was going to pee myself; I was running to the bathroom every five minutes to make sure my bladder was empty. But the funny thing was, no one else cared at all, for them it was just part of the process. That afternoon, I didn't see anyone wee themselves. But Pat said she always put on a nappy just in case!

Mike talked us through the events we would have to do on the big day and the equipment we would have to use. First, we had to get sandbags weighing 20kg then 28kg, 30kg, 38kg, and even 40 kg. We had to lift them over our head and throw them over the bar. I had never done this before, so I felt quite apprehensive. But when it was my go, everyone was very supportive.

I only managed to get to 30kg to start with, but it didn't matter. There was no negativity at all; even though it was a competition, not one of those girls put you down. It was really nice to see people helping each other out with no bitchiness. It didn't matter what you looked like; everyone had a different look and was beautiful in their own way. It was really inspiring to see how strong women could be; it's not what you are taught growing up or what you see in the media.

Next, we practised the training wheel. Here, you had to pick up a wheel with weights on and walk around in a circle with it for as long as possible; the minute you put it down, you were out. This event was tricky because, if you leant forward while lifting it, you'd fall over. I managed to walk around with it three times, carrying up to 120kg, so I was quite happy with that.

Next we tried the Viking Hold. There are two gigantic logs of 100kg each on chains and you have to hold them at arms' length for as long as you possibly can. You have two men on either side holding up the logs ready for you but when they release it, they wobble so you have to really ground yourself. I only managed to get to thirty seconds with these. Still, I gave it my best shot.

Finally, we moved on to the Atlas Stones. These are big concrete rocks which you lift and throw onto a barrel. You start with 30kg then 60kg then 70kg, 80kg, and 90kg. You have to squat down and wrap your hands around the stone then lift it up to your legs, stick out your crotch to raise it to your chest and onto the barrel. The stone is so wide, I was struggling to get my arms around it and grip it. You have to put this adhesive gel called Tacky on your hands, arms and T shirt. It's disgusting stuff, really thick and sticky, but it helps you get a grip on the stone. Trying to remove it wasn't easy though; you had to wash your hands and rub them in chalk to get it off.

Although everyone was cheering me on, I really struggled with the Atlas Stones. I couldn't even lift 30kg. Bruce encouraged me and said we'd work on it. It's hard to do at first because you need the right technique, there's a real knack to it. Still, I cheered on all the other girls, which was fun. But I don't like being defeated. That week, I was determined to practise the Atlas Stones at home, so I bought some Tack Glue. I thought was the same stuff that we had used in class, but it turns out this was actually proper glue. The tube broke and the glue spilt all over my hands and stuck my fingers together. I had to use a knife to prise my fingers apart but then I got the box stuck to my hands too. I had just got that off, when I picked up a tea towel to wipe my hands then that stuck to me too. It was a nightmare and took the whole day to come off. God, it was painful!

While I was training for Wales Strongest Woman, I heard about an event coming up in South Wales; "An Experience with Arnold Schwarzenegger." I bought tickets to go on my own straight away. I was so excited; it seemed like a sign that I was on the right path. I had always liked Arnie. Back when I was nine years old, I read his book. This was just after I'd seen the TV show *Charlie's Angels* for the first time and found out about stunt people. I was fascinated by Arnie, who was known for doing many of his own stunts. His story really moved me. He talked about how everyone doubted him at first, but he beat all the naysayers, and became a huge star.

I enjoyed the book so much, I chose it to present at a Show and Tell at school. I was thrilled to do my presentation, but everyone just sat there, twiddling their thumbs. They didn't give me any attention, but I didn't care. I was just psyched to talk about this great man and how, like him, you can achieve anything if you put your mind to it. I could relate to Arnie's experiences because everyone doubted me too. He also had plenty of rejection over the years. He wanted to go to Hollywood, but people said it would be impossible for him to become an actor because of his accent and the fact that he was too big. How wrong they were.

Now finally I had the chance to see my idol in the flesh. It was a black-tie event, so I got all dressed up in my fancy gear. I arrived early so I had the chance to meet quite a few people before the talk. I even managed to speak to the guy who founded the company that organised the event. He had always wanted to make people's dreams come true. Then one day, he had the idea; what if you could get your childhood heroes to come and speak and you could meet them? Then he read *The Secret* and that made him go for it. He had no idea how to do it, but he had the drive and ambition to try.

By now, "An Experience with ... " had turned into a huge business; he'd brought over Al Pacino, Robert De Niro, Jean Claude Van Dam, Sylvester Stallone, Mel Gibson ... the list went on and on. I was amazed to find out that this man had been inspired by *The Secret* like me. As we spoke, I told him all about my acting career and stuntwoman training, and he encouraged me to keep going.

Then I took my seat for the event. When Arnie came onstage, the crowd went wild. Before it started, you got to submit a question for Mr Schwarzenegger and luckily mine was picked. I took a deep breath; I couldn't believe that I was finally getting to talk to my childhood hero.

"Hi Arnold," I said. "Hope you're enjoying Wales!"

I told him that I was a single mum but also working as an actress and training to be a stunt woman.

"When did you get your break as I'm sure you also had times when you failed?" I asked.

Arnie was truly gracious in his reply.

"First of all, congratulations," he announced. "You are to be admired having children and having to work."

He told me that he also had five kids, so he knew how hard that was. He explained that you have to have a very clear vision of what you want to achieve. "There's no such thing as success without failure," he continued. "What makes you successful is that you have a lot of failures along the way."

He remembered when he first tried to do the bench press with five hundred pounds. "I tried ten times, I failed ten times. But I didn't conceive of myself as a failure. Because every time I failed, I got up and dusted myself off and tried again. The guys that stayed down, those were the failures. If you get up, you're a winner."

The crowd cheered as Arnie gave me a final pep talk.

"You're already up," he declared. "You're already a winner. I'm proud of you."

Wow, what an honour! I felt so blessed to have had the chance to speak to this legend. At the end of the show, I went to meet Arnie and have my picture taken with him. Once again, he revealed that he was very proud of me, especially for entering Wales's Strongest Woman. As we said goodbye, he gave me a big hug and told me to go for it.

I booked a room in a hotel for the night, which it turned out was next to Arnie's! As I was heading back there, I bumped into Eddie Hall. He was the current title holder of World's Strongest Man and good friends with Mr Schwarzenegger. Eddie and I went for a drink, and he generously took a couple of hours to talk me through everything. He said that he could see that I was a strong girl and gave me all kinds of advice from an effective diet plan to how to do dead lifts correctly. But, most of all, he told me not to quit.

The next day, I floated home on Cloud Nine. Speaking to these guys had filled me up with so much hope and given me a much-needed boost. Now I really felt that I could do it. I went back into training with a vigour like never before.

MONKEY MIND

By now, I was deep into preparing for Wales's Strongest Woman, working with my coach five nights a week. I was loving every minute, but it was very hard and intense. One night, after training, my friend Karen came to visit me.

"As you're doing that contest, you should do this one too," she announced. "I think you'd do well."

She showed me the information and it was a beauty pageant called Miss Galaxy.

"Thanks Karen but this isn't for me," I told her.

Although I'd previously gone in for Miss Loaded, I'm not really into all that beauty stuff. I'm not a girly girl, who loves hair and make-up. I'm quite laddish and more, *look at what I can do,* rather than, *look at me.*

Karen is very girly and utterly gorgeous, so I suggested she go in for it. But she wasn't having any of it. She's quite shy and doesn't like to be the centre of attention. I'm definitely the performer of us two.

"Go on," she urged. "It'll be fun."

"I don't think I look right for it," I explained. "They're all very petite. I'm not really feminine in the slightest."

"You've got it in you, Sporty Spice," Karen teased. "You could be the best Butch Miss Galaxy!"

That cracked me up. I'm not really butch but I have got big muscles. Trying to lift those damned Atlas Stones was making sure of that.

"You're pretty as well as strong," Karen insisted. "Of course, you can do it. Go on!"

But I wasn't sure. I didn't sign up and said that I had to think about it. As I went to bed that night, I had so many doubts about it that I felt physically sick. I remembered a quote from one of my many self-help books written by the spiritual teacher Ram Dass.

"One of the ego's favourite paths of resistance is to fill you with doubt."

Where was all this resistance coming from? Suddenly, I flashed back to being at school, age seven. In my mind's eye, I saw the cruel girl that pushed my head into the blackberries and ruined my best dress. Then I pictured that aggressive boy in the library who whacked my head against the table and called me ugly, whilst everyone laughed. I remembered the horror and shame that I felt, and how I just wanted the ground to open up and swallow me whole.

Then I came back to the present moment. I thought about how much work I'd done on myself and how much I've changed since my youth. I wasn't a helpless victim now. I believed that I created my own reality and filled myself with positive thoughts every day. By the morning, I had decided to do the competition just to prove to myself that I could. It was good for me to overcome my fear, plus I had nothing to lose. It was just another adventure. Why not go for it?

To apply, I had to send in images of myself dressed up in evening wear. They had to be top notch, so I enlisted my brilliant friend Ian Parker. Of all the photographers I've ever worked with, there are only a couple that I really trust. It's wonderful when you find someone like that to work with. Then you can really let go and relax, which always produces the best shots.

For the photoshoot, Ian and I went to the National Trust castle near where I live, which has beautiful, big grounds. It was a very picturesque setting and I knew Ian would get great results. But, when we started shooting, all my insecurities besieged my mind. *What the hell are you doing, Laura? You're no model any more.* On the outside I looked confident, but on the inside I was still telling myself, *There's no way you're good enough.*

After all that I'd been through, and all the self-development I'd done, it was so frustrating to still be feeling like this. But I couldn't help it. My chattering monkey mind was running riot. The negative thoughts got louder and louder until they were so deafening that I had to stop the shoot.

"I'm sorry, Ian," I whispered. "I don't think I can do this."

"What?" he gasped. "Why not?"

I trusted Ian so I told him that I didn't feel good enough. He was totally shocked.

"Why would you think that?" he protested. "You're absolutely beautiful."

But I didn't feel that way. I genuinely couldn't see what other people did. But talking my insecurities through with Ian really helped me to move beyond them. When things are in our head, they can overwhelm us; when we get them out, we can let them go.

We resumed the shoot and Ian kept encouraging me; he was so sweet. I started to relax more, and we got some really lovely images. They were totally raw – in natural light with no editing or photoshop. I wanted to use them exactly as they came out. When I got home, I uploaded them onto my application form. But when I saw the other contestants on the Miss Galaxy website, all my doubts came flooding back. *Wow, they're all so beautiful. I've got no chance.*

Resistance overwhelmed me yet again. *Maybe I should pull out of this,* I thought. The contest was triggering all of my confidence issues. Especially as I would have to go onstage in front of a room full of people in a swimsuit, alongside other girls with perfect figures who had never had kids. *There's no way I can put myself through this.*

Yet again my friends saved the day. The terrific trio Karen, Hayleigh and Gemma came around to see the pictures.

"They're gorgeous," they declared. "Just go for it and have fun!"

We had a lovely night together. I tried on all my outfits; they loved them and convinced me that the show must go on.

"You've got nothing to worry about," they declared. "It's not a big deal."

I don't think they really understood why I was feeling so insecure, but then they didn't know the extent to which I was bullied at school. They promised that they would come to the competition and support me, whatever the outcome.

"You've got friends that love you," they continued. "It doesn't matter whether you win or not."

Still, they had to admit that it takes a hell of a lot of guts to get up on stage in a swimsuit. None of them would do it. In a way, I felt like I was doing it for us all.

Before the competition, there was a grand event called the Pageant Land Ball where all the contestants got together to meet each other, have dinner, and raise money for charity. The day of the ball, I went to a professional make-up artist. She made me up and it seemed okay, but I couldn't really see what it looked like in her small mirror. However, when I got out into the street in natural light, I saw that I was bright orange. It was awful; I looked like a giant carrot!

I sent her a message saying that I liked the eyes and lips, but could she make the foundation a little lighter? Unfortunately, she took offense; she said that no one was allowed to criticise her work and told me to find a new make-up artist. I'd given her a generous tip too!

By now, it was 5.30pm and I had to leave for the ball at 6.30pm. I sent a picture of my face to Karen and she was horrified.

"You look like Donald Trump!" Karen cried. "You can't go to the ball like that. You've got to get her to change it."

I tried ringing the make-up artist, but now she wouldn't answer my calls. I went on her website and saw that all her clients had the same make up, white necks and bright orange faces. Wish I'd thought to check that before!

If I was having doubts about the competition before, now I was really getting the jitters. But I was determined not to let my monkey mind get the better of me. I went home and washed off the offending orange goo. I had to redo the foundation myself, which wasn't easy without messing up the eye make-up, but finally, I managed to fix my face – just about. I didn't look too bad, so my confidence rose a little. Cinderella would go to the ball after all.

I took a deep breath, put on my Miss Wrexham sash, and headed off to the event. It was in a big hotel in a manor house in Preston. It was very picturesque with a huge marquee in the garden and pink balloons everywhere. I walked in on my own, not knowing anyone at all. Everyone in there looked stunning; all the girls were dressed up to the nines. They were all super friendly though. I met a former contestant who gave me a few tips on how to walk onstage. Then they announced that it was time to go into the main room to eat. The woman wished me luck in the contest and walked away – very elegantly, I might add.

So I went into the ball room and joined the queue for the food. As I was waiting, I met a pretty, dark-haired girl in a red dress.

"Oh, we're in the competition together," she said, introducing herself as Sally. "It's going to be such fun!"

Sally was very kind and took me under her wing. Once we'd collected our dinner, she invited me to sit with three other girls. As we ate, they told me about themselves and how many pageants they'd done. One of them had taken part in four; although she hadn't won any, she still loved doing them and hoped that this would be her lucky year.

"Who cares anyway?" she declared. "It's not about winning. It's about coming together and raising money for charity!"

She gave a big smile and went back to her meal. When I saw her attitude, I felt ashamed about all the doubt I'd put myself through.

She's right, I thought. Who cares? I don't need to be Miss Galaxy. This is just about getting my confidence back and enjoying myself.

I couldn't believe that, two decades, five children and so many self-help books later, I was still letting those bullies at school control my life. How crazy was that? Those days were long gone. Yes, it was a horrible experience, emotionally and psychologically damaging. But, *at the end of the day, that was then, and this is now.*

I carried on chatting with the girls and tucked into my meal. Normally, I was too embarrassed in social situations and wouldn't eat in front of strangers, a hangover from my anorexia days. But there I was, stuffing my face and having a good time. We all had a great laugh, talking about what we were going to wear and how excited we were. They weren't what you'd think of as your typical pageant girls – these were strong independent women. It was very inspiring.

Sally's fiancé had left her just as they were about to get married, but she had picked herself up, brought her own beauty salon and built up a successful business. She didn't care about her ex anymore. As they say, "Don't get mad, get even!"

At the end of the night, the other girls stayed over at the hotel, but I had to go home because I was filming in London the next day. I left there feeling so happy; I had been my true self that night. Regardless of what happened with the competition, the Pageant Land Ball was a fantastic experience and really helped me. It felt great to just be me as I am, not worrying if I'm good enough or anything. As I drove home, a wave of euphoria engulfed me; all the worry had gone. As the spiritual teacher Dan Brule once said, "If you are going to doubt anything in life, doubt your own limitations." I was going to do my very best to live by those words from now on.

MISS GALAXY

I felt like I was living a double life, preparing for Miss Galaxy by day and for Wales's Strongest Woman by night. It was now the middle of February, just three weeks to the pageant. Then, annoyingly, I came down with a bad case of the flu. I was so poorly that I couldn't exercise or prepare myself in any way. I kept in touch with Sally and the other girls, who were rushing around getting ready, but I couldn't do much. I just about managed to get my outfits sorted but that was it.

Fortunately, my friend Hayleigh is a fantastic hairdresser and offered to do my hair – that's a mate you definitely don't want to fall out with! Hayleigh touched up my mane, so it was a strong, vibrant gold. I love being blonde. I first died my hair when I was nineteen because I didn't think black hair suited me. My skin is snow white with freckles, so it made me look really washed out and pale. People used to ask me if I was a Goth all the time!

I was just about over the flu by the time of the contest. It was held in a country club in Preston. Karen came with me the night before and we stayed over at the hotel. That evening, we got to meet all the other contestants and find out what they'd been doing and how much how much money they'd raised for charity. The girls were all glamorous and beautiful, but they were really lovely too. Because of the cliché of beauty pageants that you see in the movies, I was expecting them to be nasty and bitchy. But actually everyone supported one another.

"You're going to be great," they affirmed. "Just have fun and enjoy the moment."

There was no negativity; it was so refreshing. It was true friendship; there was nothing fake about it. It genuinely didn't matter if you won or not. This was about making friends for life, which is not something that I would have ever expected.

Like many people, I had thought that beauty pageants were sexist – until I entered one myself. Now I realised that the contestants aren't bimbos; they're talented professionals and entrepreneurs. All the judges were female too; one was a former Miss Great Britain, the others were local businesswomen. They got to know you to find out what you were about and what you'd done. It wasn't just about looks; you're judged on the whole package. It's much more involved than I imagined.

Karen and I had a great night, and I went to bed filled with hope for the next day. I woke up early and got ready because we had to be downstairs by 9am sharp. Some of the girls complained it was too early but that was a lie in by filming and single mum standards!

At 9am, we all met in the grand hall. It had a nice, big stage, with tables and chairs for the audience to sit in, all stylishly decorated. A former Miss Galaxy contestant acted as the compare. To get started, she introduced us and gave us a run through of what the day would be like. One by one, we were taken out of the room to have an interview with one of the four judges. There were three questions; What do you do for a living? What have you achieved? Why do you feel you are a good role model for Miss Galaxy?

When I was called for my interview, I felt nervous, but it was actually great. I told them about my career and achievements then explained that I was a good role model for women everywhere because I am a real person, a working single mum with five kids. I described how I wanted to teach women positivity and how you can achieve anything if you really believe in yourself and go for it. Just be yourself, be real.

When I came back into the room, we all got on stage to learn a dance routine. This was for the opening act when everyone comes out. Fortunately, it wasn't too complicated; we just had to walk out in a line then cross over from one side of the stage to the other. I could just about manage that – even in stilettos!

After the rehearsals, we had two hours to get ready. The hotel had a medieval banquet room, which we used as a changing room.

Everyone had their own hair and make-up artists. Hayleigh did my hair beautifully with plaits at the top and lots of long curls. I got so many compliments on it. However, the make-up artist I had booked pulled out last minute – I didn't seem to have much luck with them!

One of the girls said that her make-up artist had a free slot and could do me first. So, I sat there for half an hour getting my make-up done, while my friends went upstairs to get ready themselves. When they came back, they looked at me with total horror.

"What's wrong?" I asked.

They didn't want to say but, when the make-up artist showed me my face, I knew all too well. *Shit, they've done it again!* I thought. I looked horrendous. Not only was I bright orange, but I also had thick, massive eyebrows. What had she done to me? I'd said that I just wanted a normal looking face, but she had made me look like a bloody clown!

I paid the woman out of politeness then went outside with my friends. It was no better in natural light. Why the make-up artists decide to make you look orange nowadays, I'll never know.

"Oh my God," I cried. "Now we just have an hour to get everything ready in time."

Hayleigh gave me a cloth to quickly wipe off my make-up. I had to scrub hard to remove the big black eyebrows, which left my face all red – now I looked sunburnt! I don't wear much make up at the best of times and I'm not much good at putting it on. Unfortunately, my friends weren't either. But we all worked together, doing as best we could. Hayleigh did my eyebrows and lashes, Karen did my toenails, whilst Gemma steamed my dress for me. You know who your real friends are at times like these.

When the make-up was done, we had to put the clothes on; we literally made it with minutes before the deadline. Talk about last minute! Then we went down into the backstage room to lay out all my outfits. I had three costume changes – fashion wear, swim wear and evening wear. Suddenly, all the contestants came in, whispering to one another and offering encouragement. It was a hubbub of nerves and excitement.

The event started and everything happened so quickly. We went out and performed the opening number to an enthusiastic crowd. The hall was packed; there must have been about four hundred people there. My three musketeers were watching and giving me emotional support. It was so nice to hear them cheering when I came out. For each category, they only sent five of you out at any one time; we had to wait backstage the rest of the time. It was a bit bizarre because, to get to the stage, you had to go outside the hotel and walk around to the door on the other side of the building and enter from there. It was dark outside, and it started to rain too, so you ran the risk of looking like a drowned rat by the time you got onstage!

The first round was fashion wear, for which I wore a black, sparkly jumpsuit. It wasn't my first choice. I was going to wear bright orange shorts and a cropped top. But, before the contest, they showed a video of previous winners and Miss Teeny Bop was wearing the exact same outfit! It wasn't right for fashion wear in the adult Miss Galaxy category – I had read the wrong list. Doh! Fortunately, I had this jumpsuit as a back-up. I'd never worn it before, which was a bit risky, but it turned out fine.

Next, came beach wear; I wore a lovely, black and white checked swimming costume. I wanted to go for a bikini, but I didn't have the confidence in front of hundreds of people. So I decided to feel more comfortable and stick with the trusty one piece. This was the most nerve-wracking part for me. I don't like walking around half-naked under a spotlight in front of everyone. It was more terrifying than jumping off that hundred-foot bridge!

But I did it; I smiled and sashayed across the stage. That gave me a euphoric feeling in itself; to feel the fear and do it anyway. Not many women would have the guts to do that – especially not after having five kids. Because my surname is O'Donnell, I was at the end of the running order and called out last. It was bucketing down and freezing outside, but I still had to run around the building in my swimsuit – well, at least that was waterproof!

Finally, it was time for evening wear, which was my favourite round. I had bought a beautiful red ball gown, which I absolutely loved. Although I'd tried the dress on at home, I didn't think to walk around in it. Big mistake. When I walked around in it backstage, I realised that it was miles too big. I couldn't bloody walk in it. It was so big and heavy that it kept tripping me up. Luckily, Karen had some safety pins so she pinned up the bottom of the dress with all the netting, so I could actually move. My friends came to the rescue again – what would I do without them?

At the end of the contest, I came out in my red gown and had my moment as Belle of the Ball. Hopefully the audience couldn't see all the safety pins holding it up. Finally, the compare called everyone back on stage and read out the top ten. To my amazement, she said my name. I felt so privileged because there were a lot of really attractive, smart women on stage. The top ten had to stand at the front, then they read out the top five. I didn't make it, but I was still so happy and grateful that I'd actually gone through with it, despite all my doubts. Plus I raised £650 for a cancer charity, which made me really proud.

The new Miss Galaxy was a beautiful, thirty-one-year-old. She had done the pageant twenty times before and hadn't won so it was great that she finally had her day. After the winner was crowned, there was a party, but I had to leave early because I had an audition in London the next day. Gemma drove my friends and I home, so, to celebrate, we drank a bottle of champagne in the car. It was such fun, we were swaying and singing along to our favourite songs. I don't normally drink so I got absolutely rat-arsed!

Now I had to prepare for my next contest. I had two more weeks until Wales's Strongest Women. The training was really stepping up. Then, one day, my agent called.

"There's a TV pilot shooting in LA," she revealed. "It's a comedy drama with an English character. The producer has asked if you want to audition for the role."

I hesitated for a moment. If I got the job, it meant that I would have to pull out of Wales's Strongest Women. That would be a shame after all that training. But working as an actress in Hollywood was my lifelong dream. I didn't have to pause for long. I took a deep breath and said a big fat, "YES!"

CALIFORNIA DREAMING

The producer wanted to see me on camera, so I sent off a self-tape. Within forty-eight hours, my agent came back to me with the news – I'd got the job! I couldn't believe it, I was bouncing off the ceiling. They flew me out to LA just a few days later. It's an eleven-hour flight and the jet lag was insane. By the time I arrived, it was noon local time, whereas it was evening back home. I was completely wiped out, so I went to my hotel to check in.

I laid down in my room, but I was far too excited to sleep, as I had three days to aclimatise before I was due to film I decided to go and hit the town. I was grinning like a Cheshire cat. To begin, I wanted to see the Hollywood Hall of Fame, where they have all the stars in the pavement with the famous signatures and handprints.

I caught an uber over and had a great time looking around, thinking how amazing it was that I was finally there. There were street actors dressed up as superhero characters like Superman. One guy dressed as the Mask of Zorro came up to me.

"Normally we charge people to have a photo with them," he explained. "But can I have my picture taken with you?"

I thought that was a bit odd; maybe it was a weird chat up line but we were in La La Land so I said okay. We took the picture and afterwards, I turned around and there were crowds of Chinese people behind me.

"Picture, picture," they said, waving their phones in the air.

I guess they mistook me for a celebrity rather than someone coming to LA for the first time to shoot a pilot. It was really funny, but I wasn't in any rush, so I decided to play along. In the end, I was there for an hour getting my picture taken with hundreds of tourists on the Hollywood Walk of Fame!

I loved LA, the whole buzz of it. You never knew what you were going to see or who you were going to meet. Even though I was still aching from the flight, I went for a walk down Hollywood Boulevard. I couldn't believe my feet were now pounding this infamous street. I couldn't wipe the smile off my face, just knowing I was here. I was exhausted and exhilarated all at once.

I saw a bus that took you on a guided tour around the celebrities' houses with a guide who lets you know who's who. I decided to go for it – well, at least I wouldn't have to walk! The tour guide was hilarious, another aspiring actor, no doubt. He told us all about the history of LA then took us to the famous Hollywood sign where we all took lots of photos. It was wonderful to see such an iconic sight in real life that I had seen a thousand times on TV.

The bus drove out of the city and up some little, winding roads through the Hollywood hills. The houses up here were amazing. We saw the homes of Madonna, Tom Cruise, Britney Spears, Channing Tatum, Justin Timberlake, Katy Perry, Mick Jagger, Vinnie Jones and many more. I loved Steven Spielberg's house, which was used for the *Ironman* movies. It's on one of the highest hills in LA and has a really massive dome. But I think Sandra Bullocks' was my favourite of all. It was all white with a white gate at the front, all tucked away and hidden by the trees. It was very tasteful and stylish – just like Sandra herself.

Of course, we could only see the entrances of the houses. They had big gates on the doors and high security; we couldn't get too close. But even just being near them gave me butterflies in my stomach, just to see the houses of all these amazing actors and actresses that one day you could potentially meet or even work with. Somehow it made it all seem more real.

I did wonder how the stars felt about these bus tours of their houses though. Did they get weirded out by it? We were being shown where they live, after all. I hope stalkers don't go back after the tour and try to get a closer look. I remembered hearing about that guy Michael Fagan who broke into Buckingham palace and got all the way into the bedroom of the Queen. This looked like it would be much easier.

I loved the bus tour so much that, the next morning, I decided to go one step further and treat myself to a helicopter tour. I wanted to do something on my own just for me and I've always wanted to go in a helicopter. I got an uber from the hotel to the heliport. But the driver didn't know where the entrance was, so he just dropped me off at the side of the road. *Thanks for that,* I thought. I wandered around, unsure of where to go. There was no-one about to ask. I was in the middle of nowhere and I couldn't use my phone to call an American number. *Great, I'm completely lost. What am I going to do now?*

As I looked around, I noticed that there was a car behind me that had broken down; a really nice 4 x 4 Bentley, very smart. I went up to it and saw that the owner was fixing a flat tyre.

"Hello, can you help me?" I asked. "Do you know where this is, please?"

I showed him the name of the heliport. He gave me directions, then we got talking.

"Are you from the UK?" he guessed. Well, the accent is a bit of a giveaway. "What are you doing here?"

"I'm filming a TV pilot," I explained. "I'm an actress."

It turns out that he was in the business too.

"I work at Universal Studios," he revealed. "I cast a lot of productions."

Only in LA can you wander around lost and find a casting director at the side of the road!

The guy asked me some more about myself. When I told him about my stunt training, he explained that a friend of his was making a documentary about stunt women because they put their lives at risk yet weren't recognised for what they do.

"We could get you in on this," he declared. "He would love to have a Brit in it. You'd be great!"

Talk about being in the right place at the right time. We exchanged contact details then he gave me some industry advice, including to take some acting lessons out there. He told me to work on my American accent as the producers like you to be versatile. He gave me the number for an acting coach called Lynette McNeil. She's trained lots of stars, like Adam Sandler, Jason Lee and Ellen DeGeneres. She's a big name out there.

It was time for me to leave so we said goodbye and I finally found the heliport. The helicopter ride was fantastic; it was a massive adrenalin rush and truly another dream come true. We toured over Hollywood and saw all the stadiums and the stars' houses in Beverly Hills, even the Playboy mansion. It was amazing to have this bird's eye view of the city, which I had totally fallen in love with. *This is it,* I thought, *I'm going to bring all my kids out here. This is where I want to be!*

When I got back to the hotel, I contacted the acting coach and arranged a meeting. I took the script to her that I was going to be in, and we worked on that for a few hours. She really built up my confidence and helped me with my performance, giving me lots of ideas to try. It's always great to hear someone else's perspective on scripts, especially a professional as experienced as Lynette. Testing out the character on different levels impresses the producers and casting directors in LA. They love it when you show a range of emotions in your performance and demonstrate that the scene could be played in a number of ways.

When I worked with Lynette, she was very complimentary.

"You really have talent," she said. "And you're naturally very funny."

I was so honoured, especially coming from her as she has worked with some huge stars. Lynette offered to send my details to some agents to see if there might be someone who could represent me out there.

As well as an acting coach, I decided to get a personal trainer for the full Hollywood experience. I find that maintaining my fitness helps me stay relaxed and I feel so much better after I've worked out. On the plane over, I had met an actress who did the voices for lots of computer games. She put me in touch with her coach. In La La Land, even the voice over artists had buns of steel!

The personal trainer was called Rhino and he used to be on the British TV show *Gladiators*. My session with him was excellent and it was fascinating to hear how he managed the transition from the UK to the US. He proved it could be done and gave me lots of good tips. In general, the Brits that move to Hollywood to try and make it genuinely want to help you. It's so empowering to have that support out there.

While I was in LA, I did as much networking as I could. I had another good contact from back home. When I ran acting classes (I had to teach a subject during my teaching degree in 2019 and chose acting), I had met a guy called Nicholas who ran the hall in Oswestry that I hired for the classes. He was a photographer and used to work in film and TV. You wouldn't expect people from my local area to be so involved in the business like that, but you never know who you're going to meet – even in a town hall in Shropshire!

When I told him that I was going to LA, Nicholas put me in touch with Sandro from Blackpool who had been living out there for twenty years. Sandro is a presenter and writes books about the royals and other subjects; he's doing really well. We met up and he was so sweet, advising me on what and what not to do. All this gave me the feeling that it's not impossible to make it, you just need to be clever and find the right way in. I felt much more confident now and in the know.

All the acting and physical training was getting me so hyped up. The night before starting filming, I couldn't sleep; I was too excited. This was a big moment for me – the start of my career stateside. In the morning, I got an uber to a big studio in downtown LA. As I arrived, it was all hustle and bustle. Everyone was racing around getting stuff ready.

First of all, I went into hair and make-up. Then the director introduced me to the actor that I was working with, who's quite well known out there. We said hello then went into another room to rehearse. We got on straight away and bounced ideas off each other on how to bring out the comedy in the dialogue.

I was in two scenes, both set in a restaurant. I was playing an English woman on a mission to date American men. It was very funny and just my silly sense of humour. It's quite strange because, when I'm in the States, I sound terribly British and posh. I don't know why but I speak very correctly when I'm out there. We ran through the scenes a few times until we felt ready then went back to the director to work with him.

When we walked out on set, I was reminded just how much I love acting. The buzz when you're in costume and stand in position, in front of the cameras and the lights, the challenge of bringing a character to life and constantly pushing yourself to do better – it's one of the best feelings in the world. I'm so passionate about it that even when I think about it, my whole body goes into overdrive. I'm overwhelmed by the sense of joy.

It wasn't all glamour in Hollywood though. To be honest, I got really constipated on the plane, which carried on while I was out there. My body was completely bunged up and I felt totally exhausted.

My friend suggested that I go to get a colonic. I did some research and it seems there are no shortages of colonics in LA – guess people out there will do anything to stay slim! I made an appointment and when I arrived at the clinic, a lovely, softly spoken woman came out to greet me.

"Hi, Laura, how are you today?" she asked in her Californian drawl. "I'm going to be the one taking you through the treatment today to release a little pressure."

What a nice way of putting it. Then she gave me a big smile as if she was super happy. I was thinking, *you do know you're going to have to stick a hose in my arse and get my shit out?* I didn't say anything though – I wasn't in Wrexham now!

The lady took me through the spotless, designer clinic and into the treatment room, where she asked me to put on a gown. I did as I was told then laid down on the side on the bed. Fortunately, I was facing away from her – it would have been far too embarrassing otherwise.

As I lay there, I saw a hose pipe thing that went into a little tank on the wall, like a fish tank. I felt really nervous about what was going to happen. *Oh God, what have I let myself in for?* I thought.

Then the lady came back in the room. She seemed so excited it was as if she was going to a party or an awards ceremony. *And the prize for best poo goes to ...*

"Are you okay and ready to go?" she enquired.

"Yeah," I stammered but I didn't feel ready at all.

As she prepared the hose, I felt so awkward. I couldn't believe she had to look at people's shit all day.

"Do you like your job?" I couldn't help but ask.

"I love it," she replied, without an inch of irony. "My work is really, really helping people."

She was so serious about it, God love her. She was trying to convince me it was the best profession in the whole world. I was just trying not to laugh but then she shoved this hose up my arse. That shut me up!

"I'm now going to put in some pressure and start up the hose," she announced.

"Okay," I replied. Well, what else could I say?

She asked me if I wanted to have any vitamins in my backside too.

"Why not?" I said. "While you're up there ... "

Then the lady switched on the hose. After the water goes in, you feel your stomach go cold. It was pretty uncomfortable. They fill up your colon up with water, then they drop the pressure and your poo comes out through the tube.

By this point, I hadn't been to the toilet for three days so I was pretty packed up. It took her five or six attempts to get anything out. The machine was growling but there was nothing coming. It was like drilling for oil!

"You're tummy's very hard, isn't it?" the lady said. "But don't worry, it'll happen, I can feel it. Just breathe and it will come."

I felt like I was giving birth.

"Yes, that's it, keep breathing," she exclaimed, panting along with me.

So I huffed and puffed, whilst trying not to laugh. The more serious she became, the funnier it was.

At last, we got the first bit out.

"There it is," she cried, as though she had just seen the baby's head. "Here it comes. Well done you!"

What the hell is she on about? I thought. I was dying of embarrassment. It was horrific, but then I she told me to come back the next day because she couldn't get it all out. *Bloody hell, don't tell me I have to go through it again?*

Before I left, the lady gave me some colon cleanse tablets to soften up my stool. I had to take two the night before but, the whole experience was so frustrating that when I got back to the hotel, I decided to take two straight away and two later that night. That was a big mistake because I was shitting non-stop all night. It was one extreme to the other!

But I still went back the next day for the second colonic as it helps to remove any final debris in your colon. *Oh well, in for a penny …* I have to admit this wasn't the way I imagined spending my final night in Hollywood but there you are. I had just got my body back to normal when it was time for me to go home.

But the night before I left, I had one final adventure. I was walking back to my hotel when I passed a huge cinema. Outside were crowds of people and paparazzi – clearly someone important was about to arrive. I moved in closer and saw that this was the premiere of the Quentin Tarantino film *Once Upon A Time In Hollywood,* starring Brad Pitt and Leonardo Di Caprio. I jostled through the crowds and got right to the front, next to the red carpet.

At that moment, a big, black limo pulled up and out stepped Leo and Brad. The crowd went wild. The two stars walked along the red carpet, signing autographs and posing for photos. Everyone was screaming at them, trying to get them to look in their direction. When Leo and Brad passed me, I said hello and wished them luck with their film. Leo stopped and asked where I was from and what I was doing out there. You know how Americans love the British accent! I told him that I was an actress and had been filming. He congratulated me then headed into the cinema.

Wow, I'd been encouraged by one of the biggest stars in the world. What a fortuitous meeting and a great way to spend my last night in Hollywood. I seemed to float back to my hotel. As I strolled through the balmy Californian night, I fantasised about the time when I would be attending my own premiere and filming with Leo and Brad.

THE BRITISH CHARLIE'S ANGELS

Although I was delighted to see my kids, coming back to England wasn't easy. My heart was still in LA and I was dreaming that I was back there every night. Then, one day, I got a phone call from a performers' agent in Hollywood. Lynette, the acting coach, had spoken to her about me and she was interested in representing me.

"The thing is," the agent explained, "if we put you on our books, then you would have to move out here. Could you do that?"

Now, I had a real dilemma. I wanted to focus on my career out there, but my kids were here. I was dying to take them to LA with me but how was I going to fund it? I knew only too well that having an agent didn't guarantee that you are going to get any work. You have to have a back-up plan.

But fate soon took another twist to get me back to Hollywood. Through Nicholas, who ran the hall in Oswestry that my acting classes were in, I met a young woman called Melanie who lived in LA. She had a four-year-old son and needed some help, so my daughter Shannon went out to babysit for a month until Melanie's new nanny arrived. Shannon was eighteen by now and it was her first big trip on her own. Still, mother hen that I am, I was panicking that she was going to get lost or get on the wrong flight because she had to change at the airport. But she was an independent young woman now and had come a long way from that teenager who was too frightened to get the train back from Manchester on her own.

While Shannon was in LA, Melanie and her husband invited me to come and stay. My potential American agent said that, if I wanted to work in LA, I needed to get new head shots and a showreel done over there. It's the same for New York – you have to get different ones done in each town or they won't accept them because every place has its own style.

Now, it's expensive to pay for one set of photos – let alone three! I really wanted to get them done, but I couldn't afford it with five kids to support. A lot of what you have to do to launch your career comes down to money. It's sad really, but that's how it is. Up until then, I'd had to pay for everything myself. But this time, my parents offered to help. We sat down and spoke about what I wanted to do and what I needed. They'd seen how hard I'd worked on my career over the years, so they knew that this wasn't just a phase. They didn't have much money either, but they wanted to support me as much as they could. They knew that one day it would pay off.

"We believe in you," my dad declared. "You're so determined and hard-working. If you hadn't had the kids and had started your career when you were eighteen, you'd be famous by now!"

But you can't change the past and, of course, my children are the most important things in my life. I wouldn't choose it any other way. Now I had my PGCE so, even if I didn't make it, I was qualified to teach in the UK. To have this extra experience of working in Hollywood under my belt would be good on my CV if nothing else.

So three weeks later, I flew back to the States. My parents looked after my younger kids while I was away. I knew they'd all miss me, but they were excited for me, plus I promised to take them out there with me one day. I was in LA for a whole month, staying with Melanie and her family in Santa Monica. I helped out with the little one because Shannon was finding out just how hard looking after babies can be. My friend who is a videographer came with me for three days; his girlfriend works on the airlines, so he got a cheap flight. That's a partner you definitely don't want to break up with!

Nicholas' friend Sandro had advised me to do more videos of myself, blogging and releasing podcasts to drum up a bigger following on the web. These days, the more interest you have online, the more hireable you are. I've even heard of actresses being asked at auditions how many Twitter followers they have. My videographer friend and I started up our own little YouTube channel and documented everything that happened in LA; what I was doing and who I was with. It was like being on reality TV!

I got my headshots done like a real LA woman; it was such fun. For my American showreel, I went with a comedy and a police drama scene, in which I played a widow whose husband had just died. I went back to work with Lynette, the acting coach, on how to get into the emotion for such a sad role. Even doing the headshots and showreel was super exciting – every step I took lead me closer to my dream.

Alongside working, I wanted to let off steam and do some exercise. Every morning, about 6am, I would ride my bike along Venice beach, past all the body builders working out at the outside gym. One morning, I was cycling one way when I saw a guy cycling the other way that I recognized. I said "Hello," but a few seconds later I realised – holy shit, that's Arnold Schwarzenegger! I later found out that it was quite normal to see him around there, on the way to his gym. Unfortunately, I didn't have time to remind him that we'd already met in Wales!

Another day, I was walking along Santa Monica pier when I spotted a trapeze school. I love aerial stuff like hoops, so I thought why not give it a go? Always up for a challenge, I went to try it out. At first, you had to stretch out your body and watch a professional trapeze artist demonstrate their technique. Then you just had to go for it. You did your first swing with your legs down on the bar then you learnt how to stand up on the bar while you were swinging.

It was the first time I had ever done trapeze and it was incredible. I felt on top of the world, like I was flying through the sky. I loved the freedom of soaring through the air and doing tricks and flips. *My kids would love all this*, I thought. They're so good at gymnastics.

I also did some martial arts training. I went to the studio run by British boxer Tony Jeffries, an Olympic bronze medallist and seven times national European champion. He was such a nice guy. He told me all about how he moved to Los Angeles and wouldn't look back now – he absolutely loved it. He started his gym and created the lifestyle of which he'd always dreamed.

At Tony's gym, I did some boxing in the ring and a circuit class. It was hard work but brilliant. We were doing spinning kicks and everything, all filmed by my videographer friend for our YouTube channel. Tony had big cliental of celebrities. There were some well-known actors and actresses in my circuit class with me. I didn't recognise them but if you were American, you'd know who they were.

I loved the way that everyone seemed to look after their bodies and health in LA more than in the UK. For a lot of British guys, the only weightlifting they do is raising pints of beer to their mouths or opening a packet of crisps!

I loved Hollywood – the sunny weather, the sense of excitement in the air and the feeling that anything could happen. The only thing I didn't like was the tea. It's a nation of coffee drinkers and they really don't understand how to make a good cuppa!

There also seemed to be so much more opportunity out there. About six hundred films are shot in LA every year, compared to only about two hundred in the whole of the UK. Everyone that you met had connections to the industry and knew people who were successful. You didn't know who anyone was or who you were going to meet. It seemed that everyone was following their hearts and trying to make it. The attractive men and women who worked in the bars and restaurants were all wannabe actors. The people sitting in coffee shops were reading scripts or writing them.

Even when you popped out to the store to buy a carton of milk, you often passed people filming something or other. There were people with cameras lurking around all of the time. When you went for a stroll down Rodeo Drive, you could see these random celebrities all around. Of course, I could only afford to go window shopping on Rodeo Drive. As I drooled over the beautiful designer clothes, I thought one day that will be me. I'll be able to afford it all and bring my children out here to have the life we have always wanted.

There was a real go-getter attitude in America, where more people seemed to believe in positive thinking and manifesting their dreams. I met many others who like me had read and been influenced by *The Secret*. It really felt like I belonged there; it was the place to be. I made so many amazing connections.

Rhino, my personal trainer, recommended going to the Four Seasons hotel. It was a very fancy place, where a lot of industry people went for lunch, so you never knew who you were going to meet. In the bar, I got talking a guy who turned out to be a multi-millionaire.

"What are you doing tonight?" he asked.

I told him I had no plans, so he asked to take me out. I thought he might take me for a drink or something, but he actually invited me to go and watch the LA Lakers basketball game. We sat courtside, opposite all the celebrities like Kim Kardashian and Kanye West. Then, at halftime, we had a buffet lunch with them. I got to speak to them all.

My absolute favourite star that I met was Courteney Cox, who played Monica in the iconic sitcom *Friends*. I grew up watching that show and laughing with her, so I felt like I already knew her. It was fantastic to have a chance to chat with such an idol of mine. She was so lovely and admired the fact that I was a single mum with five kids but still out in LA, following my dreams.

Through Rhino, I also met a charming guy who was a powerful agent and came from a very wealthy family. One night, we were deciding where to have a drink.

"Where's the place to go?" I asked. "You're the local, so you decide!"

So the agent took me to Chateau Marmont, one of Hollywood's most famous hotels, frequented by the likes of Lady Gaga and U2. Completed in 1929, it's located on the infamous Sunset Boulevard and looks like an impressive, white castle. One of the most famous party sites in the world, it's the kind of place that you can't get into unless you're known – if you're not on the list, you're not coming in!

Fortunately, my agent friend was on the list and we walked in without any problems. Inside, the atmosphere was amazing. The rooms were all candle-lit and very beautiful, as were all the people. There were loads of producers, directors and actors in there and I saw lots of famous faces. It was a bit like an edition of *Vanity Fair* magazine come to life! I even met an MBA player worth thirty million who's still hassling me for a date to this day!

Then, just when I thought the night couldn't get any better, it did. After the Chateau Marmont, we went to one of my agent friend's house for an after party. We pulled up outside and it was absolutely huge. We had to go through big gates and lots of security.

"This is like a castle!" I exclaimed. "Whose house is this?"

When we walked inside, I found out; there was Leonardo de Caprio, sitting on the sofa, just chilling and having a drink. I said hello but I didn't want to hassle him – he was at home, after all. But it seemed like destiny that the last time I was in LA, I met him outside his film premiere and now here I was at his house! It seemed like a sign that I was definitely on the right track.

It seemed like I was on a roll. When I got back to the UK, I had the chance to fulfil another dream. Nina, my horse trainer, invited me to perform in a jousting show – a medieval sport on horseback where you charge at your opponent and try to knock them off their horse with your staff. I had always wanted to do jousting, ever since I saw it one year at the Anglesey Country Fair. It's so much fun but very dangerous – even King Henry 8th had a jousting accident. In 1536, age forty-four, Henry fell from his horse and was trapped beneath the animal. Some even say that his personality changed after this and he went from being fun-loving, sporty and generous to cruel, vicious and paranoid, which ultimately led to him cutting off Anne Boleyn's head. I hoped the same wouldn't happen to me!

Despite the risks, I couldn't resist signing up. I just love performing and want to do it at every opportunity – especially on horseback. I told the kids, and they were thrilled for me. They wanted to come too but they had school so I promised that they could watch next time. I arranged for the children to stay with their dads and headed to Hereford. I met with Nina and one of her stunt team riders called Katrin. She was a tall, slim lady with long dark hair, the type of person who you meet and like straight away. She was so supportive and just wanted to see you succeed, just like Nina. They had no negativity – they just wanted to build you up and were more than happy to put in the extra time to help you get where you wanted to go.

The show was part of a festival for hundreds of people, held in a massive field. There were stalls around a giant arena, where the action took place. Our performance was at midday. First, Nina came out, riding astride two horses and leaping over jumps. Wow, that was impressive. Then a male rider rose out on his horse and performed the death hang, hanging upside down off the animal as it galloped along. The crowd gasped and watched in awe.

Next, Katrin rode out. She cantered around in a circle then stood up on the horse's back and pulled Nina up over her head. I was amazed at how strong these women were. Of course, Nina and Katrin were true professionals, but I had never done a show like this before. I had learnt jousting on Nina's training course, but I had never done it in front of an audience. I was feeling very nervous but excited too. My stomach was leaping like the horses!

It was time for me to get ready, so I went into the costume tent to transform into an Arthurian knight. I wore a long black and white tunic with trousers underneath, and chain mail armour on top. This was ridiculously heavy; it felt like someone was pushing your whole body into the ground. As I got changed, I felt a surge of energy and all the stress lifted from my shoulders. I was back doing the thing I loved best.

I went outside where our horses were waiting – even they were dressed up in medieval garb. I was to ride Sunny, a gorgeous, brown stallion. I had ridden him a few times at Nina's yard and always liked him, he was so fast. Your relationship with the horse makes such a difference; if you've got a good steed, it spears you up and you're ready to take on anyone. You and the horse become one.

I said hello to Sunny and gave him a pet then jumped up to mount him. But the chain mail was so heavily, it dragged me over to the other side of his back, and I slid off. Not a great start, but I picked myself up and got back on the horse. This knight was ready for her quest!

When we were all mounted, we lined up on our horses; three women on one end versus three men on the other. Nina was called out first, along with her opponent. She quickly beat him and knocked him off his seat. The crowd cheered as he slumped down, although of course he knew how to do this safely, so he didn't hurt himself. Next, Katrin rode out and she easily beat her opponent too. As I watched them, my excitement grew almost to bursting. *I can do it*, I thought. *This is my time!*

Finally, my name was called. I lined my horse up and looked down at my target, a handsome man in his thirties. I hadn't met him before, but I'd heard that he did stunt riding for film and TV and was quite well known in that world. I pulled the lance across my arm, gave the horse a squeeze with my legs and away I went. I galloped towards my opponent and could see him getting close; he was going very fast. But before he managed to get to me, I jutted my staff towards his shoulder and gave him a push. And that was it; he was down. I had won. I couldn't believe it, I was absolutely thrilled. I felt like King Arthur himself!

To finish the show, us three girls rode around the arena doing a victory lap. It felt so amazing to be part of this powerful female team. I had become a Charlie's Angel after all!

That night, we partied like it was 1399! There was chicken roasted on the spit and a stall serving mead, a medieval fortified wine made from honey. Just as well that we couldn't drink too much because we had to return the horses. Back at the hotel, Nina, Katrin and I had our own party and went swimming in the outside pool. It was so beautiful looking over the Scottish mountains and the hills. I felt truly happy and at peace.

I came home on a high and started to plot my next adventure. My videographer and I were planning to travel all over the place to do the kind of mad stuff that people seem to love on Instagram. We were going to go back to California and perform crazy challenges like jumping off cliffs. We had it all worked out.

I felt like everything I had been through in my life had been leading up to this point – all the heartbreak that I had experienced had made me stronger and all the self-development was paying off. Now was the time that I would reap the rewards of all the struggling, it was all falling into place. *This is really going to happen,* I thought. *At last, I'm going to make it.* I could actually feel it in the air. *This is going to be my year.*

But, as they say, life is what happens when you are busy making plans. Because guess what happened next? Covid!

WHEN LIFE GIVES YOU LEMONS

Once lockdown happened, everything I had worked so hard for came to a complete stop. Obviously, I wouldn't be flying out to LA for a while. The TV pilot we had shot hadn't been fully finished and went on hold like everything else. I couldn't believe the timing of it all.

Coronavirus took away a lot of our dreams. Of course, I felt very grateful that no one I knew had contracted the virus or God forbid, died of it. But I was worried about how I was going to cope financially and professionally. I won't lie, for a moment it got me down. But then I thought about all the other struggles in my life and how I had overcome them and realised I could get through this too.

So I jumped up and put on some music. My music is really important to me and always cheers me up – upbeat music that is. If sad music comes on, I change it and play something happy instead. I like cheesy tunes, anything from the 1960s onwards. I'll dance anything with a good beat. Me and the kids would often just dance and have lots of fun. Sometimes changing your mood and perspective is as simple as that.

I tried to look at the plus side of it all. At least I got to spend a lot more time with the children because the schools were shut – along with everything else. I knew that, as a family, we were very lucky in many ways. Because we live in the countryside my family had helped support with buying a horse called Thallo in 2018 – in order to help mem train for the stunt work and soon after I got another horse too. So having the horses to look after, we were able to have lots of time out of the house, in nature, exercising. The kids definitely benefitted from lockdown in that they learnt how to ride their horses properly. We weren't sure how long it was going to last so I taught them how to cook, seeing as we couldn't go to cafes or restaurants anymore. And, of course, we always had each other – it's hard to get lonely when there are six of you in the house!

In the end, that first lockdown wasn't as bad as I thought. On the one hand, I missed dashing around filming and networking, but on the other, I loved being at home. I decided that, rather than wishing this special time away, I was going to use it wisely to think about my future and what was best for me and the children. This pause in "normal life" gave me a lot of chance to think deeply about what I wanted in my life and what was really important to me. I think the pandemic caused a lot of us to revaluate our priorities like this.

As I couldn't travel to LA or even London, I thought it would be a good idea to engage more with my local area. What was stopping me building up a base here as well? I decided to start up my own business. I applied for a grant to create my own headshot, showreel and acting company. I knew from my own career how important it was to get those sorted, but there wasn't anywhere in my area that offered a service like that.

But then my vision broadened, and I thought about including the kids. *Why don't WE think about starting our own business?* I wondered. We all love fitness and sharing our experiences with others and we've all got different skills, so why not use that? Plus it would be something for us all to focus on. This was the perfect time to demonstrate to the children that when life gives you lemons, you make lemonade not just moan that you haven't got any Coke!

I researched fitness and nutrition sites, but I didn't feel there was anything out there for us as a family. I decided that, instead of offering generic fitness for adults, I wanted a business for the whole family that would include everyone; kids, mum, dad, granny and grandad – even if they couldn't get out of their chairs. I sat down with the kids and they loved the idea. They all wanted to get involved and be in the videos. Next, we started mapping out the concept. I brought them entrepreneur books for children, and we would all sit and read them together and talk about what we had learnt about businesses. It was nice for us to have something like this to bond over as a family. Now I couldn't go away, they had my full attention, which was brilliant.

I also researched the market and looked at how I was going to get funding as a single mum of five on low income. My friend put me in touch with the Welsh government who helped me put together a business plan. Fortunately, they liked my proposal and I managed to secure a low interest loan.

Now we had the funding to get started, we started designing different logos. The first one Blake wanted was bright yellow; we were all joking about how hideous it was. The kids were in great spirits; all laughing and taking the mickey out of each other's choice, but only in a fun, friendly way, never unkind. Undeterred, we kept coming up with designs that we liked, each adding our own input. Finally, we decided on purple and blue letters on a black background. We mocked it up on the computer to see what it looked like, and we were all thrilled.

We've got a friend who does printing so he made the T shirts and hoodies for us cheaply. They were so cool! Then we got another friend to do a photoshoot. We all wore a T shirt, vest or jumper and posed together. This wasn't always easy of course. I kept telling Blake to look at the camera nicely and not pull faces, but he was getting too excited and being cheeky. He really is such a monkey!

We all had a really fun day, laughing and messing around – you can see it in the pictures. There's one of us lying down in a circle holding hands, smiling. It's like we've finally achieved something as a family. The project was bringing us closer than ever.

It made me realise that what our society is missing now is family time. Even though you see your kids, when you have to work so much, it isn't always possible to spend quality time together. We're all so busy these days. The world that we live in now is so internet orientated with phones, computers, X boxes; no one really spends time eating a family meal at the table – without any phones. The whole point of the business was to bring back the focus on spending time together. Obviously I've always put my children first, but I didn't fully realise until the pandemic how crucial this really is.

The next step was to start filming. We brought the equipment and luckily had another friend helping to film. I definitely had to pull a lot of favours on this project! I posted up an advert on Star Now for Yoga and Zumba teachers and trainers who offered exercise programmes for seniors. I looked for dieticians too. I had a circuit trainer and two friends from the gym that did Mixed Martial Arts so I got them involved. It was great to all be working together.

Once I'd picked my team, we got them in their T shirts and filmed their videos. The people that I chose had lots of talent and were passionate about what they did, which really came across on screen. I got the kids to watch the videos and they loved them. It inspired them to do their own.

Now it was the time for us to film. My friend owned a dance studio, so we started filming there. But after a couple of days, we realised that it just wasn't right. These were exercises for people to do at home after all; they were unlikely to have the space and equipment that you would find in a professional studio.

So we decided to film the rest in our home. It was great; we felt comfortable and were much more relaxed, which came across on screen. In fact, it was the perfect environment. It proved that even if you haven't got loads of space at home, there's still enough room to get active. I could even do the hula hoop in my lounge!

Ultimately, that is the message that I wanted to get across. Even though you're a mum with young kids and you can't get out, all is not lost. You can still do pre- and post-natal yoga in the sitting room or, if it's nice weather, you can go out into the garden or visit a public park. Pregnant women don't want to go to a gym, nor do most people who have just had babies. This way you don't need to pay childcare and you can do the exercise with your child. In many ways, when you start exercising, being at home is better. When they are new to fitness, a lot of people feel self-conscious, as if people are judging them and their bodies. When you're at home, you feel secure, which is so important. You can just be yourself.

Of course, most older people wouldn't even consider visiting the gym. There's a huge market for the younger generation but what about for the elders? They feel left out of fitness yet it's so important for them to keep their bodies active and stimulate their mind. All our senior fitness instructor Melinda uses for her exercises is a chair, which, as she demonstrates brilliantly, is all that you need.

At first the kids were a bit nervous in front of the camera, but they soon got used to it. Before long, they forgot we were filming, so they'd run in shouting or asking me for something to eat so we'd have to stop recording and restart.

The shoot went really smoothly. There were some really funny moments. One time, I was filming with Felicity, who was now twelve. We made a healthy drink, which only had about 150 calories. We were on camera and I said to Felicity, "Go on, Flic, you can have the first try of it."

"That would be amazing, thanks Mum," she replied and took a big mouthful.

"Is it nice?" I asked.

Felicity paused for a moment then puked up all over herself!

The drink may have been healthy, but it was absolutely vile.

Another time we were filming with Shannon. She was teaching people how to do the splits.

We turned on the camera and told her to go for it.

"There you go," she announced and immediately sunk into full splits.

I burst out laughing.

"You can't just do it like that, Shannon," I explained. "They can't already do the splits – that's the whole point. You have to show them what they have to do in order to get there."

Of course, fitness is not just physical. I wanted our project to be about more than just the body. Being in lockdown made us think a lot more about how important mental health is. Our website was aimed at the body, mind and soul. It covered every aspect of health from psychology to nutrition and was meant to be accessible for everyone.

I had suffered a lot with depression myself when I was younger because of all the bullying and abuse that I experienced. I wanted to make sure that people knew that there was help out there – you don't have to go through things alone. Too many people are suffering in silence because they are embarrassed and don't want to tell anyone what they are going through. I can't bear the thought of people feeling alone, especially kids. I want to help open their eyes to what a beautiful world we live in and change their perspective on their view of themselves and their lives.

Developing the mental health section to the website was powerful as it brought in my experience in psychology and allowed me to share what I had learnt from the struggles in my own life. In one video, we talked about narcissism. I revealed how I finally got through my relationship with my abusive ex. Another video focussed on premature babies. I discussed how Blake was born nine weeks early and the strain that was on the family, with him being in and out of hospital so much in the first five years.

I shared about how everything affected me and how I'd come through it to the other side.

I found it really hard talking about that because it was a tough time in my life but it was so worth it. It's hard when you haven't got much support to deal with experiences like this but hopefully I've helped other parents understand there is light at the end of tunnel and given them hope to carry on.

Shannon, who was now eighteen, did a video with me about being bullied at school. We discussed our experiences of both being bullied in different ways and how we've overcome it. This helps to let people know, if they are being bullied, it's just a phase of their life. It is horrible to go through, but it won't last forever. Shannon found it challenging to speak about at first, but she kept going because she wants to help people. It wasn't scripted or anything, she just spoke honestly. I was so proud of my little warrior.

Harvey and Blake did some videos about sibling rivalry. They talked about what it's like being one of five. It was hilarious because they were just squabbling more than anything. They wanted to do it but then started messing around like typical boys, even arguing about how much they loved me.

"I love Mum more that you," Harvey declared.

But Blake wasn't having it and yelled back, "No, I love Mum more!"

Turns out that they unintentionally demonstrated sibling rivalry perfectly!

THE EXTRAORDINARY O'DONNELLS

It was so cool to be working with the kids, and they were thriving, but our family fitness business didn't really take off. However we were keen to do more together and then one day I was speaking to my agent in London.

"How are things, Laura?" he asked. "What have you and the kids been up to?"

"Well, I've been teaching them how to do stunt work – how to jump ride, back flip off horses, and triple back flip."

"Wow!" he exclaimed then suddenly he had a flash of inspiration. "I've got a great idea for you."

"What's that?"

"Why don't you do a show about all these adventures with you and the kids, your crazy activities as a family? If you create a pilot for us then I can take it to the streaming companies to see if anyone's interested."

As soon as he suggested it, I absolutely loved the idea. I thought my life would make a great reality TV show; how I work in film and TV, how hectic my life is with five kids and how I've got all my family doing stunts. There isn't much on TV showing real people like that; it's usually just well-off people and pretend celebrities. I liked the fact that this would show how normal people can achieve their dreams – not just multi-millionaires!

I remembered the actor that I met in Spain who suggested I put the kids on TV. At that time, I was very resistant. I was worried about the kids being on social media in case it made them feel insecure. But when I sat down and talked to them about it, they were so excited I thought, why not? As long as they are clear about what it entails, I'll give *it a go.* Of course, I think my children are so talented that I couldn't resist showing them off a little too!

As we had previously bought the camera equipment for our fitness business idea, we were already set up. I just needed to find a director, and someone who could help me put it all together. I put up an advert up on *Star Now*. It was so funny that I was offering jobs now, not just looking for them. The poacher had turned gamekeeper!

About ten potential directors contacted me. The woman I chose lived nearby and had lots of experience. She was a drama teacher for over twenty years and directed many large-scale productions. We arranged a meeting with all the kids but because these were Covid times, we had to meet outside my house in the street!

We talked about what we were going to film, how we were going to do it, and how we were going to drum up interest in the show. The kids were so excited. When the Covid restrictions lifted, we started filming. We began by shooting the scenes with the horses. We got my trainer Nina down for the day who taught the kids horsemanship and how to look after your horses. It's not all about the stunts; these are big, beautiful creatures who need love and care too.

On the first day, I didn't do any filming. My six-year-old, black Friesian horse had done tricks before but Amelia, my ten-year-old Palomino, hadn't. Stunt work is a big change and stress for horses at first, which is hardly surprising. I think it would freak me out to have people standing on my back or hanging off me pretending to be dead!

By the end of day one, my Palomino was absolutely perfect. She was now a trick riding horse, no problem at all. On the second day, we started filming. The kids did vaulting; holding a rope and standing up on the horse, walking, trotting and cantering. We rode in pairs; I would sit on the horse then lift the kids up above my head. We also did the straight-line trick where they all lined up on the horse. They looked so sweet like that – it was like the horse-riding version of *The Sound Of Music!*

After the shoot, we edited the footage into a trailer and launched *The Extraordinary O'Donnells* Facebook page. When we put up the videos, people seemed really excited, and we got some great feedback.

"I can't wait to watch this," they posted. "It looks great!"

But then we had to stop filming for the winter. The weather was so treacherous that we couldn't do anything, and I would never put my kids or horses in any danger. Plus we were back into lockdown so that delayed everything. So there's much more to come with that show. Watch this space!

Lockdown put a temporary stop to my acting career, however there was an app I had joined called Cameo where people in the industry get celebrities to do short videos messages etc. As I already had 250,000 followers on Instagram I decided to try and make some money. I noticed that John Cleese was also on the app and I messaged him saying that I was a big fan of his and what I was doing. He gave me his email address and asked me to email privately, and then we arranged a zoom call. The first Zoom call we had he was in the USA and it was about 11pm for me. He was running late and his daughter was helping set up his computer allowing me an insight into his world without him knowing.

We chatted three or four times in the space of a few months and talked about the world and putting to rights, having general conversations. We agree that we don't seem to be able to take the micky out of ourselves any more, and it is a shame that there is no laugh out loud comedy like there used to be, everyone taking themselves too seriously. I am still in contact with him and value his support immensely.

In summer 2020, when filming started up again, I got a job playing a starring role in the TV show *Don't Stop The Music*. My character Palmer loved to sing but she was with an abusive partner. Sad to say, I had a lot of personal experience to draw on to play this role. Although I knew it would improve my performance, it was challenging for me to go inside, dig out those feelings and become that victim again.

Production started in Chester that July. I was very excited because it was a great part and I had beat a lot of competition to get it. However, I hadn't realised that it was a singing job. I know how to stay in tune but I'm not the world's strongest singer so that was pretty scary. Still, I started learning my lines and getting ready. Because we were in lockdown, my hair really needed colouring but there was nowhere that I could get it done. So I had to do the filming with bright blonde hair and jet-black roots!

Before the shoot, we all had to get a Covid test done and fortunately we were all negative. We filmed outside in the city for three days, then did the domestic scenes in a house. In one scene, I was at home, happily getting ready to go out, singing and dancing to the radio. Then my abusive boyfriend marched in and turned off the radio.

"Shut the fuck up!" he yelled. "You can't sing or dance!"

He kept putting me down until I burst into tears. It was so strange as this was almost identical to how Tom used to treat me. It was hard to go through but also very cathartic knowing that, this time, the abuse was just pretend and would stop when the director called cut.

This was my first starring role. It was so exhilarating to finally be centre stage. But then production had to stop because the theatre we were supposed to film in had to close down. Hopefully, it will be open again soon and we'll resume filming. It's a great show and I can't wait to finish it.

Unfortunately, because of Coronavirus, I also hadn't been able to pass my stunt register. But I could still perform certain stunts as long as I had qualified to a high enough level in that particular field. So I decided to film a really cool showreel to show off my skill set in fighting, horsemanship, and archery. I love the style and energy of Viking women, so I decided to create something set at that time.

I went to visit the Viking village in Telford. It looked amazing so I asked if I could use their location. They agreed; the village manager's brother even offered to help organise it all and get some extras. We had to wait for the summer, so it was safe for the horses. We came up with a simple story; an enemy would chase me on her horse and I would shoot her down with my bow and arrow. Then I'd gallop to the village to warm my people that danger was coming, which would then lead to a big battle. It was strong, sassy and dramatic – I loved it!

I needed another stunt rider, so I put up an advert. I was amazed when Molly contacted me – the woman that the sleazy horse trainer Toby had tried to set me up with in a threesome! She explained that actually, although she was training with Toby, she wasn't interested in him at all sexually; he just kept trying it on with her. Apparently, he did it with everyone. All the stuff he had told me about her fancying me was a lie; he was just trying to create a wedge between us.

So now Molly and I teamed up to do our own shows and stick two fingers up to that sleazebag. We made a pact that we were not going to let men dictate to us anymore. I think Molly and I were supposed to get back together for a reason and this was it. Finally, the sisters were doing it for themselves!

I invited Molly to come and practise on my horses. She was great and brought along her stunt saddle for trick riding. We rehearsed in the yard with my Friesian Fallo and my Palomino Amelia. The horses were incredible at the tricks. Fallo can be a bit slow and hard to get going sometimes but, on the day, she surprised us all. She just kept going and going and going, like a total pro.

I was also given a recommendation for someone who was an expert on anything Viking and did live-action role play. He had all the costumes, which he leant us for the shoot. I wore leather armour, which looked super cool, although it was really stiff to get in and out of. My friend Michelle was my make-up artist; she painted a big blue stripe down my chin like William Wallace and my hair was big and curly. When I got into the costume, I felt amazing and very powerful. Molly wore a similar outfit and loved hers too.

The day of filming finally arrived – 21 June, Summer Solstice. In the morning, we filmed at the racecourse in Oswestry. We chose this location because they have a straight galloping section which was perfect for the horse chase scene. This was Fallo's first time seeing lots of people, with all the cameras, lights and noise. Fortunately, she took everything in her stride and really went for it. When a horse builds up trust and bonds with you, you can do anything together.

I love doing action; it's so exciting and the adrenalin buzzes through your body. It's like no other feeling in the world, especially when you are doing it with your own horse, who is like your best friend.

The second half of the day was at the Viking village. There were about thirty people there who were in a Viking re-enactment group.

They were fantastic and had all the right gear. They even did everything for free; they were just happy to be a part of it. Just as well because there was no way that I could afford to pay for so many extras!

In this scene, I had to run in and warn that there were attackers coming to our village. I had to shout really loudly for them to fight. But as I screamed, it just came out as the most girly, high-pitched squeak you've ever heard. It was so funny. I had to do it several times until I sounded suitably fierce. But we got there in the end, and I loved every single second of it. It was one of the best days of my life. I felt so strong and powerful; that weak, victimised girl had gone and been replaced by a true warrioress. I felt like I could do anything now.

IF I CAN DO IT, SO CAN YOU!

Although I loved my acting and stunt work, plus all the projects with the kids, the pandemic had put everything on hold again. I was stuck once again – along with the rest of the world - and I racked my brain to think what I could do whilst I waited for things to turn back to normal.

Ever since my early days as a nurse, I've wanted to help others. I seemed to have the knack of speaking to people of all ages from all walks of life, to discover their issues and support them in finding solutions.

I still had my psychology degree and teaching qualification, but I wanted to put what I had learned into practical application. I went online and looked for courses so I could train to be a counsellor. I found an excellent one with an accredited company, for which you had to have a degree and teaching background. To get on the course, you had to do a test about the best way to deal with people. Out of fifty questions, I got 100% right. I felt that was a sign from the universe telling me that this was the right way for me to go.

This is definitely something I can do, I thought, *why not give it a try?* I didn't realise how much I would absolutely love it until I started studying. I didn't expect that it would take over my life. But, in just a few days, I had that "Aha" moment when it hit me; this is what I am meant to be doing. It was all so clear.

Learning counselling completely transformed my life once again. Most importantly, it changed the way I dealt with my children. By this point, Shannon was seventeen, Malachy was fourteen, Felicity was eleven, Harvey ten, and Blake six. Having to deal with this wide range of ages could be challenging as they were all at varied stages in their lives and had very different needs. Plus, like so many single mums, it was only me providing for them. I was the one doing it all; making sure they got up in the morning, made their beds, got ready for school. There was no one else I could rely on.

But, instead of getting stressed and overwhelmed with this responsibility, the counselling made me reinforce positivity. Instead of criticising my kids, I sat them down and talked through any problems, giving positive feedback. Through this, I found that their engagement massively improved and, now they respected me more, they were less inclined to do whatever it was again.

Increasingly, we all started working collectively and pulled together as one. I ensured that we all had designated chores in the house, and we took it from there. It was great having a big family because the big ones could assist with the little ones. Shannon, in particular, was excellent with Blake and always helped if I was late home from work. That's a God send and I'm so grateful that she's in my life, like all my kids. Yes, it's been a challenge to be a single mum of five, but it's also been such a blessing.

Once I had qualified as a counsellor, I signed up to a website called *Psychology Today*, a database where people can find the right counsellor for their needs. Fortunately, I started getting clients straight away. One was a lovely young girl of thirteen. She was sweet but had such a severe eating disorder that she could have died.

"We don't know how we can save our daughter," her mother lamented.

She explained that her daughter had been a bit bigger before lockdown, but then got too obsessed with exercise and started starving herself. She was doing two hours of spinning on the bike every day and all she would eat was carrots.

"She's just skin and bones," her mum gasped through her tears. "She's got no energy, she's going to die!"

The poor woman was absolutely at her wits end. I went around to their house, and I spoke to her parents and sister, but the girl was hiding upstairs because she didn't want to speak to me.

So I went up and spoke to her through the door to begin. Finally, she opened up and I managed to arrange a session with her. It really helped that I understood her struggle first-hand, having had an eating disorder myself when I was young and experiencing so many issues about my body.

My first meeting with the girl was to find out what she really wanted, which was an athletic body. I explained, in order to achieve that, you actually need to eat rather than just exercise. I put together a diet plan for her and took her to the shops, showing her what food to choose.

"Let's start with eating five small meals a day," I said. "And we'll progress from there."

Thank goodness she listened and followed my advice. For the first three months, she was gaining weight but not enough, so we had to cut down her cardio and up her calorie intake. Then we had setbacks because she thought the portions were too big and she couldn't do it. But through patient conversations, we managed to change her perspective and she came to realise that she could succeed after all.

Over the next three months, we progressed further; not only was she was gaining weight, we even went to having a cheat night once a week when she could eat whatever she liked. This was a huge shift for her, and her family were absolutely delighted. In the end, we signed off and shared a big Chinese take away together to celebrate.

I went home that night with a full belly and an overflowing heart. I finally felt that I was putting everything I had learned throughout my life into practise. All the struggles I had been through were worthwhile if I could support someone else through their difficulties. There is no better feeling in the world than helping someone; it's a high unlike no other. You can't put a price on that.

My next client was a woman in her mid-thirties with severe anxiety. She kept making the same mistakes over again by going back to a man who was cheating on her and abusing her. He even had a new girlfriend, and she would bump into them when she went out. They used to walk by her house every day, so she boarded up her windows so as not to see them.

When I first went to see this lady, she was very timid and nervous. I asked what she wanted, which was to be happy with herself and love herself. That has to be the ultimate goal for us all. She was unhappy with her weight too, so we spoke about diet and exercising. We started doing our sessions by going for a walk. We would have an hour and a half of walking and talking, which gave her the space to open up about her deeper issues.

Exercise helps people psychologically because their endorphins start flowing, which frees them up to talk about other issues. When you exercise, you feel better about yourself too. That's why it's recommended that we exercise three to four times a week. This improves your mood and makes you a happier person, which makes it easier to deal with life's challenges.

As well as talking through my client's problems, we came up with an exercise and diet plan. She did very well and stuck to it all. After our first session, she stopped meeting the guy and her anxiety dropped a little. After a month, she unboarded her windows and started going out more. After two months, she lost a stone in weight, so she felt more confident buying clothes. We aimed for the size she realistically could be. With regular sessions, it's easy to do. It's not a quick fix but six months is perfect. Six months can change your life.

By the end of our time together, she was her perfect size ten. More importantly, she was now concentrating on herself before she even looked at another man. Her track record before this had not been healthy; all the guys she'd been with were abusive. Because she was feeling anxious and needy, she attracted the wrong kids of partners. Now she started to think, *what do I actually want from a man?* When she was ready, she started dating again, but approaching it with this new-found self-worth. She went out confidently, with her head held high. Now she has the perfect boyfriend who worships the ground she walks on.

Another person I worked with was called Roddy. When I met him, he was not in a good place. He had been with his girlfriend for fifteen years. For the first five, everything was great, but then she started taking cocaine. Although they were still together, she treated Roddy very badly. She was just using him for money and didn't really want to be with him. He paid for her to go to rehab, but it didn't work. He found out that she was having an affair with her drug dealer. Then he discovered that she was also seeing another man that she had met in rehab, which Roddy had paid for to try and help her!

This revelation was too much for Roddy and he hit rock bottom. He was so depressed that he couldn't go to work anymore. Then it got so bad that he couldn't even get out of the front door. He had lost everything and was like a shell of a man, unable to think for himself. The lights were on, but no one was home. She had completely destroyed him.

I knew exactly how Roddy felt because this was the that I got to in my relationship with Tom. When Roddy and I started to work together, we put the focus back on him. We discussed what he wanted, what his needs were. We visualised what he desired in a partner; loyalty and commitment, someone to love him back and make him feel good about himself, and maybe even have another child. Instead of wasting his energy on someone who wouldn't give it back, he started to channel it into his children, who did love him.

Roddy was also overweight, which increased his feelings of insecurity. So we worked on his diet and found him a personal trainer. Before long, he was going to the gym three times a week. Yes, he had wobbly days when he couldn't get out of bed and felt really worthless. But on others, he was really good. We worked on changing his thought process too. Any time a negative thought came into his head, we would transform it. I'm pleased to report that Roddy is now with a lovely woman and they are expecting their first baby.

Another client was a nine-year-old girl called Lucy, who had severe ADHD. She was very quick to anger and couldn't handle herself in public situations. When she went out with her family, she would kick off all the time and scream and shout. She'd even hit her mum and push her in the river. But poor Lucy was on the receiving end of lots of aggression too. She was being bullied at school by a girl who was kicking her and telling her that she was ugly. Sound familiar? It was almost the exact situation I had been in at her age.

Together, Lucy and I started working on what she wanted out of life. The first month, we went for walks along the country path and just had a good, old chat. Her parents would be following us, but it was easier for her to talk to me as someone outside the family. We discussed how to build up her confidence. With the diagnosis of ADHD, you get labelled as a naughty child. But, in fact, she wasn't different, she was normal. She just wanted to be happy and feel included like anybody else.

ADHD gives you an impulse that you can't control so we worked on changing Lucy's thought patterns.

"Whenever you want to hit your Mum, just speak out what you want to do instead," I told her. "Say, 'I really want to push you in the water.'"

I was encouraging her to let the feelings out, but to release it in a verbal rather than a physical form. She soon got the hang of the technique and it started to work. Not long afterwards, Lucy went to a theme park with her parents and had a great day. She was off her medication at the time too, but she didn't act up at all.

Next, we worked on how she could deal with the bullies at school. I trained her to repeat in her mind that she wasn't going to get bullied anymore. It was interesting because, when she went back to school, the bully kicked Lucy but claimed that Lucy had kicked her. This time, instead of going along with it, everyone turned on the bully and knew she was lying. These days, Lucy's progressed so much that she's walking to school on her own.

I was so grateful to have been able to help Lucy. If we can help children believe in themselves early on in life, imagine how beneficial it's going to be for them growing up. The way we treat our young people is crucial. It's so important to let them have their own free thoughts and have a say in what they want to do, not just be told they can't do things all the time.

Before we could change Lucy's mind and outlook, we had to find out what her desire was so that we had the end result in view. So often, youths are coming out of school with no idea of what they want to do so they just get a job they hate, which can lead to frustration, depression and even physical illness. However, if they had a clear idea of what they wanted to do from the get-go, they would thrive in their industry. Without that end goal, you can easily get stuck in life. You have to have that desire, so you can go for it and then you can overcome almost any obstacle. I'm living proof of that!

Along with counselling, I did further training as a life coach, which gave me more skills on how to use your mind to create the life you want. I discovered that these techniques are followed by so many celebrities. Jim Carrey, Morgan Freeman, Will Self – they all achieved their dreams by using their thoughts and actions to shape their reality. If they can use these techniques to get to the top, anyone can.

These simple tools can help you manifest the life you want, in true abundance. Some people think that money is the be all and end all but, of course, it isn't. Money is just the tool to get what you want. True abundance is happiness, spending quality time with your friends and family and doing work that fulfils your soul, whilst bringing in the material resources you need. When you see how you can manifest with the power of your mind and understand the real meaning of the law of attraction, it's true freedom.

If people understood what they could achieve, there would be so many more happy, successful folk out there, which would lead to a better society. Everyone has the potential to do well in life but you have to discover your true passion and find your niche. It's so important to clarify what we are genuinely passionate about and take a chance of doing something that we love instead of failing at what we don't.

There's always going to be some risk in life but why gamble your happiness on a job you are stuck in, and ultimately hate? Always trust your gut instincts and do what you feel is best for you. When you work on what you're good at, the universe seems to bring the right people to help you on your way. You don't know what path is going to open, anything can happen. We all have it in us to do well, it's just whether you believe that you can and then have the discipline to follow through on your vision. That's where having a coach can be invaluable, a guide who has been there and can help to keep you on the path.

Life Coaching helped to solidify what I had always instinctively believed. It was an epiphany as I realised that I could combine all of the things I loved including public speaking, acting, helping people and psychology. I felt as if my whole life had been preparing me for this; I was more passionate about it than anything else.

When I had completed my training, I launched my own business called *Valkyrie Academy*, named after those powerful, female spirits of Norse mythology. I loved the name because it encapsulated that strength and determination of the warrior. I was so grateful to be helping people and that my clients were having such breakthroughs. It was like my whole life clicked into place and everything I had seen and learnt finally came together. I knew that this was my calling in life.

Everyone needs help once in a while. Even the strongest people in the world need support sometimes. I've worked with people from all walks of life, even celebrities. You might think that famous people have their lives sorted, but that can be very far from the truth. I worked with one actress who was beautiful and successful, but she felt so lonely. Many stars feel isolated because they don't have anyone that can trust. Their friends have gone to the press and stabbed them in the back for money. Even family members are out for what they can get. They can't walk out the door without the press hounding them and they receive abuse from trolls online.

I worked with this lady to get to the root of her issues. We mapped her mind and reprogrammed the way she thought. We got her to visualise what she really wanted – a loving partner and friendship group. Then we cut all of the negative people from her life; we literally went through and deleted them from her phone. When she focused on the things that she wanted and surrounded herself with the right people, she became happy. She was free to be herself and it didn't matter what the press said about her because everyone loved her for who she truly was.

I also offered life coaching in businesses settings. I worked with a sales department where, although their staff had been trained, they weren't motivated to make any sales. So we worked with them for several weeks to show them how to communicate with people effectively. Salespeople can become disheartened if they don't make any sales; they can get the negative programme in their mind that they can't sell anything then get into a downward spiral. With our techniques, we were able to remap their thinking and help them turn it around. They started making more sales again, which in turn gave them more confidence to succeed.

I haven't given up on my dream of acting and being a stunt woman, and when the world opens up again, I will be right back on that, with the backup of my counselling and life coaching business between roles. I don't have to be restricted to one career – and can get the best out of both.

People often say to me, "You're such an inspiration, how do you do it?"

They don't know how I fit it all in. But if you really manage your time, you can do it all and achieve anything you want. Yes, it's hard being a single mum to five kids and raising a family alone. It can be so challenging to keep the house clean, cook healthy meals and make sure the kids get a good education. And, of course, I'm only human. Sometimes I think that I can't keep going, but I have to show the kids something to look up to. I can't just give up – what kind of message is that?

I believe that nothing is ever really out of reach – and manifesting or setting goals in important – but that only works if you are prepared to put in the work to make it happen. You can dream of winning the lottery, but if you don't actually buy a ticket, it is not going to magically transpire. Being unstuck is freeing yourself to live your dreams and I had been stuck for 20 years because my parents didn't know any better.

I know that life is a struggle, especially when you have a family to support. I had to learn everything the hard way; nothing was handed to me on a plate. But I'm grateful for that because it has made me stronger. It's also made me living proof that anyone can do it. I get messages all the time from people who recognise how I have overcome my challenges, which is helping to improve their lives too.

There's still so much I want to do, and I know I can if I set my mind to it. All the struggles have been worthwhile as they made me who I am today. Sometimes I think back to that little girl watching *Charlie's Angels* on TV and pinch myself. I can't believe how far I've come, all the things that I've seen and done. Learning to love myself hasn't been easy. But I can honestly say, it's the most important journey that any of us will ever take.

Printed in Great Britain
by Amazon

76718676R00116